Quips, Squibs
and Some Curiosities

Leon Zeldis

Quips, Squibs and Some Curiositiess
by Leon Zeldis

Published by Cornerstone Book Publishers
An imprint of Michael Poll Publishing
Copyright © 2008 by Leon Zeldis

Cornerstone Book Publishers
New Orleans, LA

First Cornerstone Edition - 2008

www.cornerstonepublishers.com

ISBN: 1613421745
ISBN-13: 978-1-61342-174-1

MADE IN THE USA

Foreword, Warning and Disclaimer

This is not an ordinary dictionary of quotations. It is not comprehensive. I cannot vouch for the accuracy or origin of the thoughts I have collected here. I make no claim for scholarship. My guiding principle in making my choices has been: *Se non e Vero, e bene trovato*, which freely translated means: even if not true, it's well said.

I classified the quotations by subject. Some may be pigeonholed under two or more subjects. If you find the same quotation repeated, that's the reason, not a desire to fatten this little book. I enjoyed each of these observations so much, I don't want you to miss any.

The selections have been collected in the course of many years. I tried to copy them as accurately as I could but, as I said, attributions may be wrong. In many cases, I didn't find the author, so I just put them down without mentioning any name. I don't bother to write "anonymous", because the author may be known, but not by me.

Some observations are mine. I put them at the end of each subject, to make it easier to skip them over if you are not interested in my thoughts.

I have included some items that just tickled my fancy, not really quotations. Excuse me. Author's privilege.

I believe these aphorisms and thoughts to be amusing, or thought-provoking, or both. I hope you agree with my judgment. Enjoy!

Leon Zeldis

A fine quotation is a diamond in the hand of a
man of wit and a pebble in the hand of a fool.
Joseph Roux (1725-1793)

A collection of anecdotes and maxims is the
greatest treasure for a man of the world.
Wolfgang von Goethe (1749-1832)

I quote others only the better to express myself.
Michel E. de Montaigne (1533-1592)

Some for renown, on scraps of learning dote,
And think they grow immortal as they quote.
Edward Young (1683-1765)

*Quips, Squibs
and Some Curiosities*

ABSENCE

Absence extinguishes small passions and increases great ones, as the wind will blow out a candle, and blow in a fire.
La Rochefoucauld (1613-1680)

ACTION

We become just by performing just actions, temperate by performing temperate actions, brave by performing brave actions.
Aristotle (384-322 BCE)

No man does anything for a single motive.
Samuel Taylor Coleridge (1772-1834)

We would often be ashamed of our finest actions if the world understood all the motives which produced them.
La Rochefoucauld (1613-1680)

Nobody made a greater mistake than he who did nothing because he could do only a little.
Edmund Burke (1729-1797)

Eyesight is of no avail if the heart is blind.
Hebrew saying

I do not believe in a fate that falls on men however they act, but I do believe in a fate that falls on men unless they act.
Gilbert Keith Chesterton (1874-1936)

Trust no future, however pleasant!
Let the dead past bury its dead!
Act, act in the living Present!
Heart within and God overhead.
Henry Wadsworth Longfellow (1807-1882)

Action and faith enslave thought, both of them in order not to be troubled or inconvenienced by reflection, criticism and doubt.
Henri Frédéric Amiel (1821-1881)

Without passion man is a mere latent force and possibility, like the flint which awaits the shock of the iron before it can give forth its spark.
Henri F. Amiel (1821-1881)

For purposes of action nothing is more powerful that narrowness of thought combined with the energy of will.
> *Henri Frédéric Amiel (1821-1881)*
> *[cf. the hammer and chisel of Masonic symbolism]*

It is easier to stay out than to get out.
> *Mark Twain (1835-1910)*

A man would do nothing if he waited until he could do it so well that no one could find fault.
> *John Henry, Cardinal Newman (1801-1890)*

Chemists at least can use analysis; patients suffering from an illness whose cause is unknown to them can call in a doctor; criminal cases are more or less cleared up by the examining magistrate. But for the disconcerting actions of our fellow men, we rarely discover the motive.
> *Marcel Proust (1871-1922)*

The difference between perseverance and obstinacy is that one comes from a strong will and the other from a strong won't.
> *Henry W. Beecher (1813-1887)*

There is nothing more frightening than ignorance in action.
> *Johann von Goethe (1749-1832)*

A lot of men are like wheelbarrows - no good unless pushed.

However: Men are like spaghetti, you can pull them, but not push them.

Think globally; act locally.

ACTORS

An actor is a sculptor who carves in snow.
> *Ascribed to both Lawrence Barret (1838-1891) and Edwin Booth (1833-1893)*

No pen or pencil can the Actor save.
The art, and artist, share one common grave.
> *David Garrick (1717-1779)*

Acting consists in the ability to keep an audience from coughing.
> *Jean-Louis Barrault (1910-1994)*

2

She runs the gamut of emotions from A to B.
> *Dorothy Parker (1893-1967), on Katherine Hepburn*

A walking X-ray.
> *Oscar Levant (1906-1972) on Audrey Hepburn*

I never said all actors are cattle. What I said was all actors should be treated like cattle.
> *Alfred Hitchcock (1899-1980)*

Rex Harrison was notoriously rude. Once he refused an old lady his authograph outside the stage door, at which she hit him with her program, prompting Stanley Holloway to remark that, "For once, the fan hit the shit".

ADVERSITY

Sweet are the uses of adversity
which, like the toad, ugly and venomous,
wears yet a precious jewel in his head.
> *William Shakespeare (1564-1616)*

ADVICE

Be wary of the man who urges an action in which himself incurs no risk.
> *Joaquin Setanti*

It is easier to stay out than to get out.
> *Mark Twain (1835-1910)*

Sound advice is 99 percent sound and 1 percent advice.
> *Bessie and Beulah*

If God had consulted me before embarking on the Creation, I would have suggested something simpler.
> *King Alfonso X the Wise of Castille (1221-1284)*

If the stock market experts were so expert, they would be buying stock, not selling advice.
> *Norman R. Augustine (1935-   )*

How is it possible to expect that mankind will take advice, when they will not so much as take warning?
> *Jonathan Swift (1667-1745)*

Nature has given us two ears but only one mouth.
Benjamin Disraeli (1804-1881)

Severities should be dealt out all at once, that by their suddenness they may give less offence; benefits should be handed out drop by drop, that they may be relished the more.
Niccolo Machiavelli (1469-1527)

Do pleasant things yourself, but unpleasant ones through others.
Baltasar Gracián (1601-1658)

In dealing with cunning persons, we must ever consider their ends to interpret their speeches; and it is good to say little to them, and that which they least look for.
Francis Bacon (1561-1626)

In essentials, unity; in non-essentials, liberty; and in all things, charity.
John Wesley (1703-1791)

Do nothing that is not useful.
Keiko Yamanaka (1970-)

Every single day one should listen to a little song, read a good poem, look at a fine painting and, if possible, say a few sensible words.
Johann W. von Goethe (1749-1832)

When you are faced with two alternatives
Choose both.
Robert Crawford (1959 -)

Let him that would move the world first move himself.
Socrates (469-399 BCE)

I have found the best way to give advice to your children is to find out what they want and then advise them to do it.
Harry S. Truman (1884-1972)

We can give advice, but we cannot give the wisdom to profit by it.
La Rochefoucauld (1613-1680)

When you want to test the depth of a stream, don't use both feet.
Chinese proverb

You are alive so celebrate every moment.
Cherish good people, including yourself.
Get negative people out of your life.
Like a bird, soar the updrafts.
Leave a heritage so that when you die, you will be missed.
Dr. Sami Sunchild

Always drink upstream from the herd.
Will Rogers (1879-1935)

Never play poker with a man called Doc; never eat at a restaurant called Mom's, and never sleep with a woman whose problems are worse than your own.
Nelson Algren (1909-1981)

Three things cannot be brought back:
A stone, after being thrown.
A word, after being pronounced.
Time, after it has passed.

Advice is what we ask for when we already know the answer but wish we didn't.

The early bird may get the worm, but the second mouse gets the cheese.

When you starve with a tiger, the tiger starves last.

If things appear easy, it's because we didn't hear all the instructions.

Be the judge in a duel, the trainer in the army, the commentator in politics, the umpire in a game, the art critic, and the professor in everything else.
Leon Zeldis

AFTER-DINNER SPEECH

There are two things that are more difficult than making an after-dinner speech: climbing a wall which is leaning toward you and kissing a girl who is leaning away from you.
Winston Churchill (1874-1965)

It usually takes more than three weeks to prepare a good impromptu speech.
Mark Twain (1835-1910)

To talk well and eloquently is a very great art, but an equally great one is to know the right moment to stop.
>*Wolfgang Amadeus Mozart (1756-1791)*

During the French Revolution, a Doctor, a Lawyer and an Engineer were arrested together and sentenced to the guillotine. The Doctor walked up, put his head on the block, the blade fell down – and stuck! The executioner said, "That's an act of God; you are free to go!", and the Doctor said "Praise God!" and left. The Lawyer walked up, put his head on the block – and the same thing happened. He said, "Praise God!" and left. The Engineer walked up to the block, looked at the guillotine – turned to the executioner, and said "You know, if you'd just put a drop of oil up there…".

AGING see also OLD AGE

Old age is the rarest of things in a palace.
>*Lucius Annaeus Seneca (4 BCE – 65 CE)*
>*[He should know. Had to commit suicide at the behest of Nero. LZ]*

Man dies too soon to be able to know immortal things.
>*Seneca (4 BCE – 65 CE)*

The hardest years in life are those between ten and seventy.
>*Helen Hayes (1900-1993), at 73*

At my age, flowers scare me.
>*George Burns (1896-1996)*

Intellectual blemishes, like facial ones, grow more prominent with age.
>*La Rochefoucauld (1613-1680)*

When people tell you how young you look, they are also telling you how old you are.
>*Cary Grant (1904-1986)*

Whoever coined the "Golden Years" slogan was a man in his twenties.
>*Dr. Israel Drapkin*

A man is not old until regrets take the place of dreams.
>*John Barrymore (1882-1942)*

The flower in the vase still smiles, but no longer laughs.
>*Malcolm de Chazal (1902-1981)*

Maturity is the age when you are still young, but with much more effort.
Jean Louis Barrault (1910-1994)

Years steal the fire from the mind as vigour from the limb,
And life's enchanted cup but sparkles near the brim.
Lord Byron (1788-1824)

Youth is a blunder; manhood a struggle; old age a regret.
Benjamin Disraeli (1804-1881)

Age imprints more wrinkles in the mind than it does on the face.
Michel de Montaigne (1533-1592)

Aging is the only way not to die.

Old age is full of surprises, most of them unpleasant.

Like paper, the soul withers, and turns dry, crackly and wrinkled.
Leon Zeldis

ALUMINUM

Aluminum is the fourth most common element on Earth, yet its existentece wasn't even suspected until 1808, when it was discovered by Humphrey Davy.

AMBASSADOR

An ambassador is an honest man sent abroad to lie for his country.
Sir Henry Wotton (1568-1639)

AMBER

In the early 18th century amber was more than ten times more valuable than gold. When, in 1681, the Great Elector Frederich Wilhelm sent a throne made of amber to the Tsar Theodor III, he called it "the greatest curiosity in the world". But the most extraordinary use of the precious resin was the "Amber Room", an entire chamber made up of finely worked amber panels that would glow in candlelight, built for the first King of Prussia, Frederick I, after his coronation in Königsberg in 1701. It disappeared after the Second World War.
Catherine Scott-Clark and Adrian Levy

AMBITION

Ambition is the last refuge of failure.
> *Oscar Wilde (1854-1900)*

The slave has but one master; the ambitious man has as many as can help in making his fortune.
> *La Bruyére (1645-1696)*

Ambition, like scratching, can never be satisfied.
> *Leon Zeldis*

AMERICA

Some 80 percent of Americans say they believe in angels.
> *T. M. Luhrmann (1959 -   )*

The English are polite by telling lies. The Americans are polite by telling the truth.
> *Malcolm Bradbury (1932-2000)*

The American people never carry an umbrella. They prepare to walk in eternal sunshine.
> *Alfred E. Smith (1873-1944)*

The worst country to be poor in is America,
> *Arnold Toynbee (1889-1975)*

One should never visit America for the first time.
> *Jawaharlal Nehru (1889-1964)*

In California everyone goes to a therapist, is a therapist or is a therapist going to a therapist.
> *Truman Capote (1924-1984)*

Thought is barred in this city of Deadful Joy, and conversation is unknown.
> *Aldous Huxley (1894-1963) on Los Angeles*

War is God's way of teaching Americans geography.
> *Ambrose Bierce (1842-1914)*

America: toilet paper too thin, newspapers too fat.
> *Winston Churchill (1874-1965)*

Sir, they are a race of convicts and ought to be grateful for anything we allow them short of hanging.
> *Dr. Samuel Johnson (1709-1784), on Americans*

America is a land where a citizen will cross the ocean to fight for democracy - and won't cross the street to vote in a national election.
> *Bill Vaughan (1872-1958)*

The big cities of America are becoming Third World countries.
> *Nora Ephron (1941-)*

In San Francisco, Halloween is redundant.
> *Will Durant (1885-1981)*

Oh to be in L.A. when the polyethyl-vinyl trees are in bloom!
> *Herb Gold (1924-)*

All of our political institutions and cultural institutions have been unsually geared toward commercial activity, and you can see that part of the success of hucksters comes from this idea, whether it is patent medicine or a new religion, that you are selling the possibility of transformation.
> *Bruce J. Shulman*

Americans: People who laugh at African witch doctors and spend 100 million dollars on fake reducing systems.
> *Leonard Louis Levinson*

The discovery of America was the occasion of the greatest outburst of cruelty and reckless greed known in history.
> *Joseph Conrad (1857-1924)*

Americans are always eager to entertain conspiracy theories. They flourish in the artificially nourishing soil of academe, immune to scientific reasoning and logical discourse.
> *Mary Lefkowitz (1935-)*

Los Angeles: many suburbs in search of a city.

The English like to hunt foxes; Americans hunt witches. Since there are none to be found, they invent them, giving them different names each time.
> *Leon Zeldis*

Americans are hated because they are so successful and so generous. Success provokes envy, and generosity breeds greed.
Leon Zeldis

ANALOGY

Analogy is the highest function of imagination, combining analysis and synthesis, translation and creation.
Charles Baudelaire (1821-1867)

Most reasoning, or metaphysical, religious, esthetic, scientific, historical postulates, are made analogically. Analogical thought is transcendent, extrapolating, compared to analytical thought, which is syllogistic. It is selective, and capable of 'foreseeing'. The syllogistic technique, on the contrary, is composed of tautologies, or better, 'truisms', obtained by substitutions and eliminations.
Dorothy Emmet (1904-2000), quoted by Matila Ghyka (1881-1965)

Analogies are misleading, like linking ants with elephants because they share some of the DNA.
Leon Zeldis

ANARCHIST

The anarchist... is disappointed with the future as well as the past.
Gilbert Keith Chesterton (1874-1936)

The anarchist thinks that demolishing a house he'll be able to build a better one with the rubble.
Leon Zeldis

ANGELS

The human species would never produce a race of angels; genes for wings and for moral character are not present in human populations.
J.B.S. Haldane (1892-1964)
In heaven an angel is nobody in particular.
George Bernard Shaw (1856-1950)

Some 80 percent of Americans say they believe in angels.
T. M. Luhrmann (1959-   )

ANGER see **BAD TEMPER**

10

ANTS

Ants have lived for more than 80 million years, while man's civilization is scarcely more than 7000 years old. They are the oldest cosmopolites; they have sheltered longest, grown food, escaped many of the violences of the mammalian world. Have they changed? It would seem they have changed very little if at all. They are one of the small "immortals". They attained their present relatively high biological specialization very long ago and have since been marking time or evolving so slowly that the modifications are extremely small.
Loren C. Eiseley (1907-1977)

ANXIETY

Anxiety is the interest paid on trouble before it is due.
William R. Inge (1860-1954)

Hire paranoids. Even though they have a high false alarm rate, they discover all plots.
Herman Kahn (1922-1983)

We cannot control events in our external world, but we have the ability to control how we view these events and the emotional response we choose to have to them.
Patty Wooten

We suffer primarily not from our vices or our weaknesses, but from our illusions. We are haunted, not by reality, but by those images we have put in place of reality.
Daniel J. Boorstin (1914-2004)

Anxiety is excitement without oxygen.

Whistling in the dark may not be advisable; it attracts predators.
Leon Zeldis

APATHY

The tyranny of a prince in an oligarchy is not so dangerous to the public welfare as the apathy of a citizen in a democracy.
Montesquieu (1689-1755)

In Germany they came first for the Communists, and I didn't speak up because I wasn't a Communist. Then they came for the Jews, and I didn't speak up because I wasn't a Jew. Then they came for the trade unionists, and I didn't speak up because I wasn't a trade unionist. Then they came for the Catholics, and I didn't speak up because I was a Protestant. Then they came for me, and by that time no one was left to speak up.
    Martin Niemoeller (1892-1984)

APPEARANCES

In all things, circumstance is required as well as substance. The first thing we meet is not the essence of things but their appearance; from the exterior we arrive to the knowledge of the interior.
    Baltasar Gracián y Morales (1601-1658)

If you look good and dress well, you don't need a purpose in life.
    Robert Pante

Our greatest pretenses are built up not to hide the evil and ugly in us, but our emptiness. The hardest thing to hide is something that is not there.
    Eric Hoffer (1902-1983)

Only God helps the badly dressed.
    Spanish proverb

Though it may dress in silk, the monkey is still a monkey.
    Spanish proverb

Every man has his secret sorrows which the world knows not - and often times we call a man cold, when he is only sad.
    Henry Wadsworth Longfellow (1807-1882)

The great majority of mankind are satisfied with appearances, as though they were realities, and are often even more influenced by the things that seem than by those that are.
    Niccolo Machiavelli (1469-1527)

Sometimes when you look in his eyes you get the feeling that someone else is driving.
    David Letterman (1947-   )

It is only shallow people who do not judge by appearances.
    Oscar Wilde (1854-1900)

Clothes make the man. Naked people have little or no influence on society.

Sincerity is the key to life; once you can fake that, you've got it made.

There is sin in sincerity.
  Leon Zeldis

APPEASEMENT

Appeasement is feeding your friends to a crocodile in the hope the you will be the last to be eaten.
  Sir Winston Churchill (1874-1965)

ARCHITECTURE

A doctor can bury his mistakes but an architect can only advise his client to plant vines.
  Frank Lloyd Wright (1869-1959)

ARGENTINE

If I had not been born Perón, I would have liked to be Perón.
  Juan Perón (1895-1974)

Argentineans are Spanish-speaking Italians.

ARGUMENTS

Arguments are to be avoided; they are always vulgar and often convincing.
  Oscar Wilde (1854-1900)

I never make the mistake of arguing with people for whose opinions I have no respect.
  Edward Gibbon (1737-1794)

A liberal is a man too broadminded to take his own side in a quarrel.
  Robert Frost (1874-1963)

One must destroy the seriousness of an opponent with laughter, and his laughter with seriousness.
  Gorgias (483-378 BCE)

If you cannot convince them, confuse them.
> *Harry S. Truman (1884-1972)*

When you have no basis for an argument, abuse the plaintiff.
> *Marcus Tullius Cicero (106-43 BCE)*

It is not necessary to understand things in order to argue about them.
> *Caron de Beaumarchais (1732-1799)*

Arguments only confirm people in their own opinions.
> *Booth Tarkington (1869-1946)*

The first human who hurled an insult instead of a stone was the founder of civilization.
> *Sigmund Freud (1856-1939)*

Don't argue wth a fool. The spectators can't tell the difference.
> *Charles Nalin*

Positive: being mistaken at the top of one's voice.
> *Ambrose Bierce (1842-1914)*

We are not satisfied to be right, unless we can prove others to be quite wrong.
> *William Hazlitt (1778-1830)*

There are two theories to arguing with women. Neither one works.

Children's games end in a fight; grown-up's fights end in a game.
> *Leon Zeldis*

ARROGANCE

Arrogance is truly tantamount to idolatry.
> *The Talmud*

Academic and aristocratic people live in such uncommon atmosphere that common sense can rarely reach them.
> *Samuel Butler (1835-1902)*

If other people are going to talk, conversation becomes impossible.
> *James McNeill Whistler (1834-1903)*

We are the first race of the world, and the more of the world we inherit the better it is for the human race.
> *Cecil Rhodes (1853-1902)*

ART and ARTISTS

A great work of art is like a dream; for all its apparent obviousness it does not explain itself and is always ambiguous.
> *Carl Jung (1875-1961)*

Art for art's sake makes no more sense than gin for gin's sake.
> *Somerset Maugham (1874-1965)*

Skill without imagination is craftsmanship and gives us many useful things such as wickerwork picnic baskets. Imagination without skill gives us modern art.
> *Tom Stoppard (1937-   )*

I have finished the chapel I have been painting. The Pope is very well satisfied.
> *Michelangelo (1475-1564), writing to his father after finishing the Sistine Chapel frescos.*

Quality is art's equivalent for the truth.
> *Robert Aron (1898-1975)*

Art is the perfection of nature.
> *Thomas Browne (1605-1682)*

If it were not for the intellectual snobs who pay, the arts would perish with their starving practitioners – let us thank heaven for hypocrisy.
> *Aldous Huxley (1894-1963)*

Creative activity could be described as a type of learning process where teacher and pupil are located in the same individual.
> *Arthur Koestler (1905-1983)*

Mirrors serve to see one's face; art, to see one's soul.
> *George Bernard Shaw(1856 – 1950)*

Art is the expression of man's pleasure in labor.
> *William Morris (1834-1896)*

A work of art is not execution. A work of art is revelation.
> *Louis Calaferte (1928-1994)*

A man who works with his hands is a laborer; a man who works with his hands and his brain is a craftsman, but a man who works with his hands, his brain and his heart is an artist.
> *Louis Nizer, (1902-1994)*

Art is the lie that enables us to approach truth. From art's point of view, there are no concrete or abstract shapes, but only more or less conventional interpretations.
> *Pablo Picasso (1881-1973)*

Art is the language of the beautiful.
> *Adolphe Pictet (1799-1875), Swiss polymath, credited with being the first to prove that the Celtic languages belong to the Indo-European family.*

Ads are the cave art of the twentieth century.
> *Marshall McLuhan (1911-1980)*

I shut my eyes in order to see.
> *Paul Cézanne (1839-1906)*

With an apple, I will astound Paris.
> *Paul Cézanne (1839-1906)*

Rodin's art is beefsteak and muscle.
> *Constantin Brancusi (1876-1957), Rumanian sculptor*
> *[Yet he also said that he couldn't work in Rodin's studio, because nothing grows well beneath a great tree. LZ]*

Art, like morality, consists in drawing the line somewhere.
> *G. K. Chesterton (1874-1936)*

Either it is easy, or is impossible.
> *Victor Hugo (1802-1885)*
Bad artists always admire each other's work.
> *Oscar Wilde (1854-1900)*

Make art your slave, not your owner and master.
> *Wong Shun Leung (1935-1997)*

Art is what makes visible the *nature* of things.
> *Rudolf Arnheim (1904-2007)*

Though I recognize that the observation of reality is necessary, true art lies in the reality that is felt.
> *Odilon Redon (1840-1916)*

Art is I, science is we.
> *Claude Bernard (1813-1878)*

The true artist is the one who dialogues with his work; the impostor dialogues with the public.
> *Ernst Gombrich (1909-2001)*

The aim of art is to represent not the outward appearance of things, but their inward significance.
> *Aristotle (384-322 BCE)*

A man paints with his brains and not with his hands.
> *Michelangelo (1475-1564)*

It is a shame that in Venice they never learned to draw well from the beginning.
> *Michelangelo (1475-1564), after visiting Titian in his study, quoted by Vasari*

Art is not a mirror to reflect the world, but a hammer with which to shape it.
> *Vladimir Mayakovsky (1893-1930)*

Art is a natural defense against pessimism.
> *Friedrich Nietzsche (1844-1900)*
> *[and yet, not a few artists went mad. LZ]*

Abstract art: a product of the untalented, sold by the unprincipled to the utterly bewildered.
> *Al Capp (1909-1979)*

There is no abstract art. You must always start with something.
> *Pablo Picasso (1881-1973)*

It does not matter how badly you paint so long as you don't paint badly like other people.
> *George Moore (1852-1933)*

Arts offer intimations of eternity.
> *George Steiner (1929-   )*

To be deprived of art and left alone with philosophy is to be close to hell.
Igor Stravinsky (1882-1971)

The best critic is the one who writes from the work of art, rather than about it.
Octavio Paz (1914-1998)

The artistic life is a long and lovely suicide, and I am sorry that it is so.
Oscar Wilde (1854-1900)

Art lies in concealing art. (*Ars est celare artem*)
Ovid (43 BCE – 18 CE)

In our secular age, museums are being turned more and more into temples and artists into prophets.
Ian Buruma (1951-   )

Freud once listed the artist's spurs as fame, money and the love of women.
Joseph Rykwert (1926-   )

Great moments in art follow in the wake of the invention of new media, when artists have not fully assimilated them.
Edmond Duranty (1833-1880)

In Botticelli's paintings the human figure always has to hold its own against the emptiness of the world.
Damian Dombrowski

Much art today has abandoned the ambition to please the viewer aesthetically. Instead, it seeks to shock, discommode, repulse, proselytize, or startle.
Roger Kimball (1953-   )

He bores me. He ought to have stuck to his flying machines.
August Renoir (1841-1919), about Leonardo da Vinci

The deepest dimensions of man (life, death) can be transmitted in no other language than that of metaphor, that of poetry, that of art.
Mario Irarrázaval (1940-   )

The language of art is silence.
Mario Irarrázaval (1940-   )

Once Degas witnessed one of his paintings sold at auction for $100,000. Asked how he felt, he said: 'I feel as a horse must feel when the beautiful cup is given to the jockey.'

Michelangelo put horns on the head of Moses in his famour statute of the Hebrew leader, because of the erroneous translation of the Bible made by Jerome, the 'Vulgata'. He took the Hebrew word *karan* to mean 'horned', when it actually meant 'beamed' or 'radiated'.

You cannot eat and sing at the same time.
Leon Zeldis

Mixing colors, like mixing words, if not done in the right proportions results in a muddy chaos.
Leon Zeldis

ATHEISM

An atheist is a man who has no invisible means of support.
John Buchan (1875-1940)

I once wanted to become an atheist but I gave up. They have no holidays.
Henry Youngman (1906-1998)

Atheism is a non-prophet organization.

Atheism is the religion of the morally challenged.
Leon Zeldis

AUTHORITY

It is dangerous to be right in matters on which the established authorities are wrong.
Voltaire (1694-1778)

The tyranny of a prince in an oligarchy is not so dangerous to the public welfare as the apathy of ta citizen in a democracy.
Montesquieu (1689-1755)

Authority has every reason to fear the skeptic, for authority can rarely survive in the face of doubt.
Robert Lindner

BAD LUCK

If I dealt in candles, the sun would never set.
> *Yiddish proverb*

I have a rock garden. Last week three of them died.
> *Richard Tiran*

If all our misfortunes were laid in one common heap whence everyone must take an equal portion, most people would be contented to take their own and depart.
> *Socrates (470?-399 BCE)*

Even misfortune gets tired.
> *Seneca (4 BCE- 65 CE)*

All of us have sufficient fortitude to bear the misfortunes of others.
> *La Rochefoucauld (1613-1680)*

In China, you must not let your own shadow slip into an open casket or a grave. If it does, you'll die soon after.

BAD TEMPER

Whoever is in a rage resembles an idolater.
> *Saying of the Hebrew Sages [cf. Arrogance]*

Anger is a brief madness.
> *Horace (65-8 BCE)*

Speak when you are angry, and you will make the best speech you will ever regret.
> *Ambrose Bierce (1842-1914)*

Don't try to get rid of a bad temper by losing it.
Keep honking while I reload.

BEAUTY

Beauty is symbol.
> *Plotinus (205-270)*

The beautiful is the symbol of the morally good.
> *ImmanuelKant (1724-1804)*

Beauty is the purgation of superfluities.
Michelangelo (1475-1564)

A delight in beauty is linked to a love of freedom.
Leigh Hunt (1784-1859)

A beautiful object is one that grips our faculties, offering disinterested pleasure.
Immanuel Kant (1724-1804)

Rarely do great beauty and great virtue dwell together.
Francesco Petrarca (1304-1374)

A thing of beauty is a joy forever.
John Keats (1791-1825)

The most beautiful things in the world are also the most useless; peacocks and lilies, for example.
John Ruskin (1819-1900)

It is a sad thing to think of, but there is no doubt that Genius lasts longer than Beauty.
Oscar Wilde (1854-1900)

Statesmen and beauties are very rarely sensible to the gradations of their decay.
Earl of Chesterfield (1694-1773)

I'm tired of all this nonsense about beauty being only skin-deep. That's deep enough. What do you want - and adorable pancreas?
Jean Kerr (1922-2003)

Some years ago, *New Scientist* invited readers to propose Standard International units for beauty. A "Helen" was the most popular suggestion, with a "milli-Helen" defined as enough beauty to launch a single ship.
Dr. Thomas Dormandy

Justice is to God as beauty is to man.

I was so ugly when I was born that the doctor slapped my mother.

In Latin-derived languages, similar words define beauty and good:

Bello e buono, Belle et bon, Bello y bueno.
Also in other languages:
Latin: *pulcher* = good and beautiful.
Greek: *kalos* (from Sanskrit *kalyas*): healthy, agreeable, beautiful
Hebrew: *yafeh* = beautiful, good.
>   *Leon Zeldis*

BEES

For many centuries, nobody knew where bees came from. Aristotle didn't
know and Virgil praised them for their abstention from sexual
intercourse. In 1260, Canon Thomas of Cantimpré insisted bees practiced
Christian chastity and told monks they could learn from bees.
>   *Hettie Ellis*

BEING

Thinking and being are the same thing.
>   *Parmenides (5ᵗʰ century BCE)*

Lord, we know what we are, but know not what we may be.
>   *William Shakespeare (1564-1616)*

BELIEF

Man's most valuable trait is a judicious sense of what not to believe.
>   *Euripides (c. 495-406 BCE)*

Though a good deal is too strange to be believed, nothing is too strange to
have happened.
>   *Thomas Hardy (1840-1928)*

I believe because it is absurd (*Credo quia absurdum*).
>   *Attributed to Saint Augustine (354-430)*

Never believe anything until it has been officially denied.
>   *Claud Cockburn (1904-1981)*

I respect your faith but doubt is what gets you an education.
>   *Wilson Mizner (1876-1933)*

My preferences are subjective, because I am a subject, not an object.
>   *Miguel de Unamuno (1864-1936)*

The fact that a believer is happier than a skeptic is no more to the point that the fact that a drunken man is happier than a sober one.
George Bernard Shaw (1856-1950)

Desire engenders belief.
Marcel Proust (1871-1922)

Alas, reason is not effective against faith, or against searched for miracles by the desperate.
Dr. Michael B. Shimkin (1913-1989)

Every man prefers belief to the exercise of judgment.
Seneca (4 BCE - 65 CE)

The public will believe anything so long as it is not founded on truth.
Edith Sitwell (1887-1964)

Absolute faith corrups as absolutely as absolute power.
Eric Hoffer, philosopher (1902-1983)

Faith, like virginity, once lost cannot be recovered.
Pi y Margall (1824-1901)

Convictions are more dangerous enemies of truth than lies.
Friedrich Nietzsche (1844-1900)

I would never die for my beliefs, because I might be wrong.
Bertrand Russell (1872-1970)

To one who has faith, no explanation is necessary; to one without faith, no explanation is possible.
St. Thomas Aquinas (1225?-74)

I believe because it is impossible. (*Credo quia impossibile*)
Attributed to Tertullian (160?-230?)

If the work of God could be comprehended by reason, it would be no longer wonderful, and faith would have no merit if reason provided proof.
Pope Gregory I (The Great) (540-604)

Many things are too strange to be believed, but nothing is too strange to have happened.
Thomas Hardy (1840-1928)

We are not going to stop believing in something just because it has become incredible.
Robert Frost (1874-1963)

The majority of mankind is lazy-minded, incurious, absorbed in vanities, and tepid in emotion, and is therefore incapable of either much doubt or much faith.
T. S. Eliot (1888-1965)

Faith is believing what you know ain't so.
A schoolboy, quoted by Mark Twain (1835-1910)

It is surely one of the curious paradoxes of history that science, which professionally has little to do with faith, owes its origins to an act of faith, that the universe can be rationally interpreted, and that science today is sustained by that assumption.
Loren C. Eiseley (1907-1977)

BIGOTRY

The mind of a bigot is like the pupil of the eye; the more light you pour upon it, the more it will contract.
Oliver W. Holmes, Jr. (1841-1935)

Thew door of a bigoted mind open outwards so that the only result of the pressure of facts on it is to close it more tightly.
Ogden Nash (1902-1971)

I don't feel we did wrong in taking this great country from them [the Indians]. There were great numbers of people who needed new land, and the Indians were selfishly trying to keep it for themselves.
John Wayne (1907-1979)

If we believe absurdities we shall commit atrocities.
Voltaire (1694-1778)

Prejudice, not being founded on reason, cannot be removed by argument.
Samuel Johnson (1709-1784)

The nearest to a Negro is a Sambo, the next a Mulatto, next a Quadroon, next a Mustee, next a Mustiphino, after which the shade is lost, for children of a Mustiphino, by a white man, are accounted white by law.
Rev. R. Bickell, writing in 1825

BIOLOGY

Biology grows on you.
> *Frank Gioffrida*

BIRTH CONTROL

We all worry about the population explosion, but we don't worry about it at the right time.
> *Arthur Hoppe*

Whenever I hear people discussing birth control, I always remember that I was the fifth.
> *Clarence Darrow (1857-1938)*

BLOOPERS

Virgin's interest boosts 'super jumbo' prospects.
> *Financial Times, 2.5.2003*

After an access cover has been secured by 16 hold-down screws it will be discovered that the gasket has been omitted.
> *De la Lastra's Corollary*

The loss of life will be irreplaceable.
> *Dan Quayle (1947 -   )*

We are ready for any unforeseen event that may or may not occur.
> *Dan Quayle (1947-   )*

Beethoven, who had ten children, practiced on a spinster in the attic.
> *Attributed to the Philadelphia Bulletin*

BODY AND SOUL

The soul is the wife of the body. They do not have the same kind of pleasure or, at least, they seldom enjoy it at the same time.
> *Paul Valéry (1871-1945) [in other words, physical pleasure and intellectual enjoyment seldom go together. LZ]*

If God wanted me to touch my toes, He would have put them on my knees.

The molecular structure of the brain is incredibly unstable. A recent study showed that every molecule making up the region around a synapse – the junction between two brain cells where subtle alteration is supposed to lock in a memory – is being replaced by the hour. Some molecules need replacing every few minutes. So much for the brain as a repository of memories that might sit untouched for decades. The brain you had even last year will have been rebuilt many times over by now.

BOOKS

These are not books, lumps of lifeless paper, but minds alive on the shelves.
> *Gilbert Highet (1906-1978)*

No place affords a more striking conviction of the vanity of human hopes than a public library, for who can see the wall crowded on every side by mighty volumes, the works of laborious meditations and accurate inquiry, now scarcely known but by the catalogue.
> *Dr. Samuel Johnson (1707-1784)*

Discretion is not the better part of biography.
> *Lytton Strachey (1880-1932)*

When I get a little money, I buy books; and if any is left, I buy food and clothes.
> *Desiderius Erasmus (1465-1536)*

Whoever has two pairs of pants should sell one and buy this book.
> *Georg Christoph Lichtenberg (1742-1799)*

Books have led some to learning and others to madness.
> *Francesco Petrarca (1304-1374)*

The road to ignorance is paved with good editions.
> *George Bernard Shaw (1856-1950)*

I am a part of all that I have read.
> *John Kieran (1892-1981)*

Macedonio Fernández says that long visits are short at the beginning. I don't think so. Long visits are too long from the beginning, and they keep being so, even if they last chronologically no more than a few minutes. The same happens with books.
> *Jorge Luis Borges (1899-1986)*

This is not a book to be cast aside lightly, it should be hurled with great force.
>   *Dorothy Parker (1893-1967)*

Thank you for sending me a copy of your book – I'll waste no time in reading it.
>   *Moses Hadas (1900-1966)*

This book fills a much-needed gap.
>   *Moses Hadas (1900-1966)*

If someone handed you a book and said, 'Read it, it will change your life', you'd probably run like hell.
>   *Normal Mailer (1923-2007)*

I took a course on speed reading and was able to read 'War and Peace' in twenty minutes. It's about Russia.
>   *Woody Allen (1935-   )*

Some books are to be tasted, others to be swallowed, and some few to be chewed and digested.
>   *Francis Bacon (1561-1626)*

A book is the cognitive equivalent of a looking-glass. The stronger our thoughts, the clearer the image.
>   *Harold Bloom (1930-   )*

No two persons ever read the same book.
>   *Edmund Wilson (1895-1972)*

In literature as in love, we are astonished at what is chosen by others.
>   *André Maurois (1885-1967)*

A good way to start a library is to leave out the works of Jane Austen.
>   *Mark Twain (1835-1910)*

Nothing is said that has not been said before.
>   *Terence (185-159 BCE)*

Euripides was mocked by his fellow citizens for keeping a library.
>   *Erich Segal (1937-   )*

Books are good enough in their own way, but they are a mighty bloodless substitute for life.
>   *Robert Louis Stevenson (1850-1894)*

Do not read to contradict or refute, nor to believe and accept by condescension, but to weigh and evaluate.
Francis Bacon (1561-1626)

A novel is like marriage; a short story is like an affair, a beautiful week-end.
Russell Banks (1940-   )

The dirtiest book of all is the expurgated book.
Walt Whitman (1819-1892)

The newspaper is the natural enemy of the book, as the whore is of the decent woman,
The Goncourt Brothers, (1823-1896 and 1830-1870)

A man may as well expect to grow stronger by always eating as wiser by always reading.
Jeremy Collier (1650-1726)

To read without reflecting is like eating without digesting.
Edmund Burke (1729-1797)

All books hold a promise; few fulfill it.
Leon Zeldis

BOREDOM

Being bored is an insult to oneself.
Jules Renard (1864-1910)

Mankind is apparently doomed to vacillate eternally between the extremes of distress and boredom.
Arthur Schopenhauer (1788-1860)

Macedonio Fernández says that long visits are short at the beginning. I don't think so. Long visits are too long from the beginning, and they keep being so, even if they last chronologically no more than a few minutes. The same happens with books.
Jorge Luis Borges (1899-1986)

BUDDHISM

The true target the archer must point to is his heart.
Kyudo maxim

Oneself does evil, oneself suffers, oneself avoids evil, oneself is purified. Purity and impurity are things of oneself, no one can purify another.
Buddha (563?-453? BCE)

An act of pure love is worth more than a lifetime dedicated to make offerings to the gods.
Buddha (563?-453? BCE)

The Eightfold Path: Right view, right aim, right speech, right action, right living, right effort, right mindfulness, right contemplation.

BUILDING

My precept to all who build is, that the owner should be an ornament to the house, and not the house to the owner.
Cicero (106-43 BCE)

BUREAUCRACY

Bureaucracy is a giant mechanism operated by pygmies.
Honoré de Balzac (1799-1850)

The only thing that saves us from bureaucracy is its inefficiency.

BUSINESS

Business is a combination of war and sport.
André Maurois (1885-1967)

Don't sell the steak, sell the sizzle.
Marketing slogan

First rate people hire other first rate people. Second rate people hire third rate people. Third rate people hire fifth rate people.
André Weil (1906-1998)

A blind beggar had a sign saying 'I'm blind, please help me'. Donations were few. An advertising man came by, changed the sign, and the beggar started receiving a bounty of alms. The sign said: 'It's spring, and I can't see it'.

An ethical businessman is as rare as a panda, and has about the same chances of survival.
>   *Leon Zeldis*

CALUMNY

Calumny is like counterfeit money: many people who would not coin it circulate it without qualms.
>   *Diane de Poitiers (1499-1566)*

Lead, when molded into bullets, is not so mortal as when founded into letters.
>   *Andrew Marvell (1621-1678)*

The Hebrew sages told that a malicious word is more dangerous than a dagger, for a dagger can injure only those who are near, while malicious words can injure those far away.

CANADA

Canada has never been a melting pot; more like a tossed salad.
>   *Arnold Edinborough (1922-2006)*

When they said Canada, I thought it would be up in the mountains somewhere.
>   *Marilyn Monroe (1926-1962)*
>   *[She made a fortune playing the dumb blonde. LZ]*

CANCER

Cancer is a word, not a sentence.

CAPITALISM

The fear of capitalism has compelled socialism to widen freedom, and the fear of socialism has compelled capitalism to increase equality.
>   *Will (1885-1982) and Ariel Durant (1898-1981)*

The inherent vice of capitalism is the unequal sharing of the blessings. The inherent blessing of socialism is the equal sharing of misery.
>   *Sir Winston Churchill (1874-1965)*

One of the things capitalism brought into the world was democracy, though I do not think the two are inseparable.
> *Michael Harrington (1928-1989)*

Under capitalism man exploits man; under socialism the reverse is true.

CHANCE

Chance is perhaps the pseudonym of God when He did not want to sign.
> *Anatole France (1844-1924)*

The generation of random numbers is too important to be left to chance.

CHANGE

The human mind treats a new idea the way the body treats a strange protein; it rejects it.
> *P.D. Medawart*

If you dislike change, you're going to dislike being irrelevant even more.
> *Eric Shinseki*

The forces that make for change are always more important for the future, and therefore in restrospect they seem at the time signs of the instability of the prevailing order.
> *Chris Wickham*

If we want things to stay as they are, they will have to change.
> *Giuseppe Tomasi di Lampedusa (1896-1957)*

The world changed much more rapidly than men. The human being remains faithful to himself. In his passions, his fears, his anxiety and his despair, men recognize themselves in a huge mirror where life and death are part of the same process.
> *Osvaldo Quiroga*

It is not the strongest of the species that survive, nor the most intelligent, but the one most responsive to change.
> *Charles Darwin (1809-1892)*

The only way to change the systems and to improve governments is to change and improve man himself.
> *José Valdemar Portillo López*

Change does not necessarily assure progress, but progress implacably requires change. Education is essential to change, for education creates both new wants and the ability to satisfy them
> *Henry Steele Commager (1902-1998)*

Every generation laughs at the old fashions, but follows religiously the new.
> *Henry David Thoreau (1817-1862)*

Change is the end result of all true learning.
> *Leo Buscaglia (1924-1998)*

There is nothing permanent except change.
> *Heraclitus (540-475? BCE)*

Change is inevitable, except from a vending machine.

CHARACTER

Nearly all men can stand adversity, but if you want to test a man's character, give him power.
> *Abraham Lincoln (1809-1865)*

A man's defects are the faults of his time while his virtues are his own.
> *Johann W. von Goethe (1749-1832)*

Let us say not, 'Every man is the architect of his own fortune', but let us say, 'Every man is the architect of his own character'.
> *George Dana Boardman (1801-1831)*

Fortune does not change men, it unmasks them
> *Suzanne Necker (1739-1794)*

The test of every religious, political, or education system is the man that it forms.
> *Henri F. Amiel (1821-1881)*

One can acquire everything in solitude except character.
> *Stendhal (1783-1842)*

Reading makes a full man, meditation a profound man, discourse a clear man.
> *Benjamin Franklin (1706-1790)*

The child is father to the man.
> *William Wordsworth (1770-1850)*

Character is destiny.
> *Heraclitus (540-475? BCE)*

Thoughts lead to purposes; purposes go forth into actions; actions form habits; habits form character; and character fixes our destiny.
> *Tyron Edwards (1809-1894)*

The reasons which any man offers to you for his own conduct betray his opinion of your character.
> *Sir Arthur Helps (1813-1875)*

When someone behaves like a beast, he says "After all, one is only human." But when he is treated like a beast, he says: "After all, one is human."
> *Karl Kraus (1874-1936)*

If the only tool you have is a hammer, you tend to see every problem as a nail.
> *Abraham Maslow (1908-1970)*

I'm as pure as the driven slush.
> *Tallulah Bankhead (1903-1968)*

Swans have an air of being proud, stupid and mischievous - three qualities that go well together.
> *Denis Diderot (1713-1784)*

A man has three characters: that which he exhibits, that which he has, and that which he thinks he has.
> *Alphonse Karr (1808-1890)*

There is an eagle in me that wants to soar and there is also a hippopotamus in me that wants to wallow in mud.
> *Carl Sandburg (1878-1967)*

Only a man of strong character can admit he was wrong. Politicians never do.
> *Leon Zeldis*

The sum total of a man is constant: the higher he climbs, the smaller he becomes.
Leon Zeldis

CHARITY

Charity creates a multitude of sins.
Oscar Wilde (1854-1900)

Blessed are those who can give without remembering and take without forgetting.
Elizabeth Bibesco (1897-1945)
[taken from Seneca. LZ]

Too many have dispensed with generosity in order to practice charity.
Albert Camus (1913-1960)

Charity will never be true charity unless it takes justice into account.
Pope Pius XI (1857-1939)

Mitzvot (religious commands to "do good") must be fulfilled in thought, speech and deed, parallel to *Beriah, Yetzirah* and *Asiyah,* respectfully.
[These are the three worlds of Cabbala. Cf. the three ways to recognize a Mason, by signs, token and words. LZ]

The highest form of charity is education.
Leon Zeldis

CHESS

Chess is as elaborate a waste of human intelligence as you can find outside an advertising agency.
Raymond Chandler (1888-1959)

CHICAGO

I think that's how Chicago got started. A bunch of people in New York said, 'Gee, I'm enjoying the crime and the poverty, but it just isn't cold enough. Let's go west.'
Richard Jeni (1957-2007)

CINEMA see MOVIES

CHILDREN

I like children if they're properly cooked.
> *W. C. Fields (1880-1946)*
> *[an echo of Swift. LZ]*

Children are aliens. And we treat them as such.
> *Ralph W. Emerson (1803-1882)*

All children as essentially criminal.
> *Denis Diderot (1713-1784)*

The trouble with children is that they are not returnable.
> *Quentin Crisp (1908-1999)*

A child tells in the street what its father and mother say at home
> *The Talmud*

Children begin by loving their parents. After a time they judge them. Rarely, if ever, do they forgive them.
> *Oscar Wilde (1854-1900)*

When a mother hasn't enough will power to discipline her children, she calls her weakness child psychology.
> *Dr. Laurence J. Peter (1919-1990)*

Insanity is hereditary, you can get it from your children.
> *Sam Levenson (1911-1980)*

The reason grandparents and grandchildren get along so well is that they have a common enemy.
> *Sam Levenson (1911-1980)*

When a father gives to his son, both laugh; when a son gives to his father, both cry.
> *Yiddish proverb*

Most of us become parents long before we have stopped being children.
> *Mignon McLaughlin (1913-1983)*

If in the past the child was dressed as an adult, now it is the adult who dresses as a child.
> *Juan Goytisolo (1931-   )*

Grandchildren are God's reward for not killing your own children.

Be nice to your kids. They will choose your nursing home one day.

CIVILIZATION

The first human who hurled an insult instead of a stone was the founder of civilization.
Sigmund Freud (1856-1939)

Civilization is nothing else but the attempt to reduce force to being the last resort.
José Ortega y Gasset (1883-1955)

Barbarism is never finally conquered; given propitious circumstances, men and women who seem quite orderly will commit every conceivable atrocity.
Evelyn Waugh (1903-1966)

The Modern world is essentially a Technicolor version of one of those Dürer woodcuts in which the knightly rider is flanked by death and the Devil in his journey through a landscape ravaged by war and plague.
Peter Porter (1929-   )

The whole history of civilization is strewn with creeds and institutions which were invaluable at first and deadly afterwards.
Walter Bagehot (1826-1877)

To accept civilization as it is practically means accepting decay.
George Orwell (1903-1950)

Civilization is a page written on one side with the pen and on the other side with the sword.
Alphonse Esquirós (1812-1876)

Science has done more for the development of western civilization in one hundred years than Christianity did in eighteen hundred years.
John Burroughs (1837-1921)

The more civilized a people is, the greater is its respect for life and the value given to human life.
Editorial, Libertad Digital (Internet newspaper), *17.10.2003*

The notion of primitive man possessing some inner peace which we civilized people have somehow lost, and need to regain, is a lot of nonesense. Your average New Guinea native lives not only in fear of his enemies, but in terror-struck dread of the unknown.
> *Gordon Linsley*
> *[So much for Rousseau. LZ]*

The only true hope for civilization [is] the conviction of the individual that his inner life can affect outward events and that, whether or not he does so, he is responsible for them.
> *Stephen Spender (1909-1995)*

You can't say that civilization doesn't advance, for in every war they kill you a new way.
> *Will Rogers (1879-1935)*

It is so stupid of modern civilization to have given up believing in the devil when he is the only explanation of it.
> *Ronald Knox (1888-1957)*

When Albert Schweitzer returned from a visit to England after a long stay in Africa, he was asked, "Well, what do you think of civilization?" He replied, "It's a good idea. Somebody ought to try it."

COEXISTENCE

You can't shake hands with a clenched fist.
> *Indira Gandhi (1917-1984)*

Let us pray, that come it may,
And come it will for a' that,
That man to man the whole world o'er
Shall brothers be for a' that.
> *Robert Burns (1759-1796)*

COFFEE

The first coffee shop was opened in Byzantium (Istanbul) in 1554, and the first coffeehouse in England opened in 1650 at the Angel Inn in Oxford (owned by a Jew named Jacob), followed by another in London two years later. By 1663 there were over eighty coffeehouses in London, which grew to over a thousand by the end of the century. Coffeehouses emerged alongside alehouses as centers of sociability, of business (auctions of art and books were held in them) and of gossip. Most importantly, it has been argued, they became the major exchanges of news and political debate and the salons of an emerging bourgeois public sphere that transformed the nature of public life.

Brian Cowan

In 1675, King Charles II issued a proclamation banning coffee houses, because they might spread sedition.

Cocoa was introduced in Europe in the 19th century.

COINCIDENCE

In Chester, Pennsylvania, a man named John McCafferty was arrested in June 1949 as a vagrant. McCafferty insisted the police was wrong, claiming he had a home, at 714 McIlvane Street. Tell it to the judge, the police said. McCafferty duly appeared before Magistrate R. Robinson Lowry, who asked him where he got that address.
'It's just an address,' McCafferty replied.
'I'll say it is,' responded the judge. That's where I live.'

Richard Blodgett

On August 19, 1939, identical twin boys were born in Piqua, Ohio, and given up for adoption separately. Both were named Jim by their adoptive families, the Lewises and the Springers. When the Jims were reunited for the first time 40 years later, they discovered that each had married a woman named Linda, divorced her and remarried a woman names Betty. Lewis had named his first son James Alan, Springer had named his James Allan. Both had childhood dogs named Toy. The brothers drank the same brand of beer, smoke the same brand of cigarettes and drove the same make of car.

Peter Watson (1943-   )

Five thousand copies of Steinbeck's novel *The Wayward Bus* were destroyed by fire when the truck carrying them from the bindery was involved in a collision. The cause of the accident was a wayward bus traveling on the wrong side of the road.

Book-of-the-Month Club News, *May 1947*

The odds are better than 50-50 that among a group of 23 people chosen at random, at least two will have identical birthdays.

The strange coincidences of Lincoln and Kennedy:

> LINCOLN was elected in 1860, KENNEDY in 1960.
> Both had legality of election contested.
> Both were deeply involved in civil rights struggle.
> Both were slain on a Friday, in the presence of wives.
> Both wives lost a son when she was First Lady.
> Both were shot in the head from behind.
> Kennedy was shot while riding in a Lincoln made by Ford, while Lincoln was shot in Ford's Theatre.
> Both have 7 letters in their last name.
> Lincoln's secretary, named Kennedy, advised him not to go to the theater.
> Kennedy's secretary, named Lincoln, advised him not to go to Dallas.
> Their successors, both named Johnson, were southerners and had previously served in the US Senate.
> Andrew Johnson was born in 1808, Lyndon Johnson in 1908.
> John Wilkes Booth was born in 1838, Lee Harvey Oswald in 1939.
> Both Booth and Oswald were shot to death before trial could be arranged.
> Andrew Johnson, Lyndon Johnson, each contain 13 letters.
> John Wilkes Booth, Lee Harvey Oswald, each contain 15 letters.

COMMITMENT

Involvement and commitment are like ham and eggs. In ham and eggs, the chicken has an involvement. The pig is committed.
>   *Dr. Yosef Vardi*

COMMITTEE

A committee is a group that keeps minutes and loses hours.
>   *Milton Berle (1908-2002)*

If Columbus had had an advisory committee he would probably still be at the dock.
>   *Justice Arthur Goldberg (1908-1990)*

To get something done, a committee should consist of no more than three men, two of them absent.
>   *Dr. Laurence J. Peter (1919-1990)*

COMPUTERS

It's not so long ago that people thought that semiconductors were part
time orchestra leaders and microchips were very, very small snack foods.
Geraldine Ferraro (1936-)

Klington prompt: strike any user when ready.
Mental backup in progress. Do not disturb!
Multitasking: screwing up several things at once.
My Go amn keyboar oesn't have any 's.
One picture is worth 128K.
Programming is an art form that fights back.
Smith & Wesson – the ultimate "point-and-click" interface.
System has erased all work in progress. Press any key to ignore and
continue.
System has violated data integrity. Delete all data? Y/y_
The generation of random numbers is too important to be left to chance.
The reason computer chips are so small is that computers don't eat much.
THINK – it gives you something to do while the computer is down.
To define recursion, we must first define recursion.
We are Microsoft. Resistance is futile. You will be assimilated.
Error: Keyboard not attached. Press F1 to continue.
File not found. Should I fake it?
If you can knock it, it's hardware; if you can only insult it, it's software.
Failure is not an option; it comes bundled with the software.

There are 10 types of people: those who know binary and those who
don't.

CONSCIENCE

Conscience is a mother-in-law whose visit never ends.
H. L. Mencken (1880-1956)

Conscience is the inner voice that warns us that someone may be looking.
H. L. Mencken (1880-1956)

The Anglo-Saxon conscience doesn't keep you from doing what you
shouldn't; it just keeps you from enjoying it.
Salvador de Madariaga (1886-1978)

Conscience is, in most men, an anticipation of the opinion of others.
Sir Henry Taylor (1800-1886)

Thus conscience doth make cowards of us all;
and thus the native hue of resolution
is sickled o'er with the pale cast of thought.
William Shakespeare (1564-1616)

The fox condemns the trap, not himself.
William Blake (1757-1827)
[Cf. the Spanish proverb: The lame blames the pavement]

A clean conscience is a sign of bad memory.

Conscience is a cur that will let you get pass it but that you cannot keep from barking.

CONSERVATISM

We know what happens to people who stay in the middle of the road - they get run over.
Aneurin Bevan (1897-1960)

Don't worry about people stealing an idea. If it's original, you will have to ram it down their throats.
Howard Aiken (1900-1973)

He that will not apply new remedies must expect new evils, for time is the greatest innovator.
Francis Bacon (1561-1626)

The U.S. standard railroad gauge (width between the two rails) is exactly 4' 8.5". That's an exceedingly odd number. Why was that gauge used? Because that's the way they built them in England, and in the U.S. railroads were built by English expatriates.

Why did the English build them like that? Because the first rail lines were built by the same people who built the pre-railroad tramways, and that's the gauge they used, and why did they use that gauge? Because the people who built the tramways used the same jigs and tools that they used for building wagons which used that wheel spacing.

Now, why did the wagons have that particular odd wheel spacing? Because if they had used any other spacing, the wagon wheels would break in some of the old, long distance roads in England, because that's the spacing of the wheel ruts.

Who built those old rutted roads? The first long distance roads in Europe (and in England) were built by Imperial Rome for their legions. The roads have been used ever since.

And the ruts in the roads? Roman war chariots first formed the initial ruts, which everyone else had to match for fear of destroying their own wagon wheels. Since the chariots were made for (or by) Imperial Rome, they were all alike in the matter of wheel spacing.

The spacing of the wheels in the Roman chariots was just wide enough to accommodate the back ends of two war horses. So the U.S. standard railroad gauge of 4 feet and 8.5 inches derives from the original specification of Roman chariots, depending on the backside of two horses.
Michael Krugel

Special duty on playing cards was abolished in England only in 1960.

Although the whole world now uses the Centigrade scale of temperature, the United States holds on to the old Fahrenheit.

The farthing, worth ¼ of a penny, was legal tender in Great Britain until 1961.

CONTRACTS

A verbal contract isn't worth the paper it's written on.
Samuel Goldwyn (1882-1974)

CONVERSATION

The trouble with her is that she lacks the power of conversation but not the power of speech.
George Bernard Shaw (1856-1950)

He had occasional flashes of silence that made his conversation perfectly delightful.
Sydney Smith (1771-1845), on Macaulay

I can never be certain of what you will understand. As one Master forbidding his students from taking even the simplest written notes said, 'What I know is one thing; what I am able to put into words is another thing; what you hear is something else; and what you understand is something altogether different.'
Chassidic story quoted by William S. Aronstein

The meeting of two personalities is like the contact of two chemical substances: if there is any reaction both are transformed.
Carl Jung (1875-1961)

CONSPICUOUS CONSUMPTION

In England, in the second half of the 18th century, the pineapple was so rare and expensive (about £80.- or £5,000 of today) that in banquets a single fruit was used as a centerpiece on the table, and was passed from one home to another until rotten.
Fran Beauman

COUNSELING

If Columbus had had an advisory committee he would probably still be at the dock.
Justice Arthur Goldberg (1908-1990)

My greatest strength as a consultant is to be ignorant and ask a few questions.
Peter Drucker (1909-2005)

If it's free, it's advice; if you pay for it, it's counseling; if you use either one, it's a miracle.

COUNTRYSIDE

One day, a friend invited the poet Max Jacob to spend a week in the country. "The countryside?", asked the poet. "That horrible place where chicken move around raw?"

COURAGE

Courage is resistance to fear, mastery of fear - not the absence of fear.
Mark Twain (1835-1910)

Some men have acted courage who had it not, but no man can act wit.
Marquis of Halifax (1633-1695)

COWARDICE

Cowardice is seeing what is right and failing to do it.
Confucius (c. 551-479 BCE)

A frown or polite displeasure in the face of what is loathsome is cowardice.
José Marías (1965-   )

CREATION

Only work which is the product of inner compulsion can have spiritual meaning.
>   *Walter Gropius (1883-1969)*

Grass-blade is no easier to make than an oak.
>   *James Russell Lowell (1819-1891)*

Creation implies the divine act of origination, creation from nothing; invention suggests a mere assembling of available materials.
>   *George Steiner (1929-   )*

There is a coherent plan in the universe, though I don't know what the plan is for.
>   *Fred Hoyle (1915-2001)*

The secret of creativity is knowing how to hide your sources.
>   *Albert Einstein (1879-1955)*

We are all as God made us and frequently much worse.
>   *Miguel de Cervantes (1547-1616)*

Every creator painfully experiences the chasm between his inner vision and its ultimate expression.
>   *Isaac Bashevis Singer (1904-1991)*

Every composer knows the anguish and despair occasioned by forgetting ideas which one has not time to write down.
>   *Hector Berlioz (1803-1869)*
>   *[and the same goes for poets. LZ]*

CRIME

Obviously crime does pay, otherwise there'd be no crime.
>   *G. Gordon Liddy (1930-   )*

CRISIS

In Chinese writing, the word "crisis" is compose of two characters, one represents danger and the other represents opportunity.
>   *John Kennedy (1917-1963)*

If you are going through hell, keep going!
Winston Churchill (1874-1965)

Any idiot can face a crisis - it's the day to day living that wears you out.
Anton Chekhov (1860-1904)

Where there's smoke there's toast.

CRITICS

The best critic is the one who writes from the work of art, rather than about it.
Octavio Paz (1914-1998)

The good critic is that who relates the adventures of his soul among the master works.
Anatole France (1844-1924)

In criticism, the only method is to be intelligent.
T.S. Eliot (1888-1965)

A drama critic is a man who leaves no turn unstoned.
George Bernard Shaw (1856-1950)

Six minutes is the proper time to spend reading a book for review.
Oscar Wilde (1854-1900)

Never trust the artist. Trust the tale. The proper function of a critic is to save the tale from the artist who created it.
D. H. Lawrence (1885-1930)

I love criticism just so long as it's unqualified praise.
Noel Coward (1899-1973)

I never read the books I criticize. They are so prejudicial.
Sydney Smith (1771-1845)

A negative judgement is more satisfying than praise, if it emits a whiff of jealousy.
Jean Baudrillard (1929-2007)

It had only one fault. It was kind of lousy.
James Thurber (1894-1961)

This book fills a much needed gap.
>   *Moses Hadas (1900-1966)*

Critics are like eunuchs in a harem: they know how it's done, they have seen it done every day, but they are unable to do it themselves.
>   *Brendan Behan (1923-1964)*

Impersonal criticism is like an impersonal fist fight or an impersonal marriage, and as successful.
>   *George Jean Nathan (1882-1958)*

Asking a working writer what he thinks about critics is like asking a lamp-post how it feels about dogs.
>   *Christopher Hampton (1946-)*

A critic is a man who knows the way but can't drive the car.
>   *Kenneth Tynan (1927-1980)*

He bores me. He ought to have stuck to his flying machines.
>   *August Renoir (1841-1919), on Leonardo da Vinci*

That's not writing, that's typing!
>   *Truman Capote (1924-1984), on Jack Kerouac*

His imagination resembles the wings of an ostrich.
>   *Thomas B. Macaulay (1800-1859), on Dryden (1631-1700)*

He had occasional flashes of silence that made his conversation perfectly delightful.
>   *Sydney Smith (1771-1845), on Macaulay*

Henry James had a mind so fine that no idea could violate it.
>   *T. S. Eliot (1888-1965)*

Always willing to lend a helping hand to one above him.
>   *F. Scott Fitzgerald (1896-1940)*

Pay no attgention to what the critics say; there has never been set up a statute in honor of a critic.
>   *Jean Sibelius (1865-1957)*

CRUSADERS

The First Crusade... set off on its two-thousand mile journey by massacring Jews, plundering and slaughtering all the way from the Rhine to the Jordan. 'In the temple of Solomon,' wrote the ecstatic cleric Raimundus de Agiles, 'one rode in blood up to the knees and even to the horses' bridles, by the just and marvelous Judgment of God!'
Herbert J. Muller (1905-1980)

CULTURE

When I hear the work culture, I take out my gun.
Herman Goering (1893-1945)

It is madness to believe that the republican regime is possible in a nation lacking culture. Culture is the soul of the free nations.
F. and R.

Between cultivated minds, the first interview is the best.
Ralph Waldo Emerson (1803-1882)

On how many people's libraries, as on bottles from the drugstore, one might write: "For external use only."
Alphonse Daudet (1840-1897)

If modern civilized man had to kill the animals he eats, the number of vegetarians would rise astronomically.
Christian Morgenstern (1871-1914)

You will always find hatred strongest and most violent where there is the lowest degree of culture.
Johann W. von Goethe (1749-1832)
[Goethe would undoubtedly have changed his opinion after the Holocaust perpetrated by the German people, among the most cultured in the world. LZ]

CUNEIFORM

Turkish museums hold 130,000 Hittite and Mesopotamian cuneiform tablets. London's British Museum has the world's largest collection of nearly 160,000.

CURIOSITY

In order for something to become interesting, all one need do is to look at it closely enough.
> *Gustave Flaubert (1821-1880)*

The important thing is not to stop questioning. Curiosity has its own reason for existing. One cannot help but be in awe when he contemplates the mysteries of eternity, of life, of the marvelous structure of reality.
> *Albert Einstein (1879-1955)*

The whole art of teaching is only the art of awakening the natural curiosity of young minds for the purpose of satisfying it afterwards.
> *Anatole France (1844-1924)*

The cure for boredom is curiosity. There is no cure for curiosity.
> *Ellen Parr*

When curiosity turns to serious matters, it's called research.
> *Marie von Ebner-Eschenbach (1830-1916)*

CYNICISM

Cynicism is only the art of seeing things are they are instead of how they should be.
> *Oscar Wilde (1854-1900)*

A cynic is the man who knows the price of everything and the value of nothing.
> *Oscar Wilde (1854-1900)*

Cynicism is humour in ill-health.
> *H.G. Wells (1866-1946)*

Gaiety is the most outstanding feature of the Soviet Union.
> *Joseph Stalin (1879-1953)*
> *[Like claiming that hell is the most happy place. LZ]*

I hope you have not been leading a double life, pretending to be wicked, and being really good all the time. That would be hypocrisy.
> *Oscar Wilde (1854-1900)*

DANCING

Dancing is the vertical frustration of a horizontal desire.

DEATH

Dying is one thing, not living is another.
Louis Calaferte (1928-1994)

To philosophize is to learn to die.
Jacques Derrida (1920-2004)

Life is Death. Organisms live because it parts are always dying.
Claude Bernard (1813-1878)

Death less feared gives more life.
Pedro de Valdivia (1500?-1553)

An anticipatory acknowledgment of death is a condition of authenticity.
Martin Heidegger (1879-1976)

Most people would sooner die than think; in fact they do so.
Bertrand Russell (1872-1970)

I die worshipping God, loving my friends, not hating my enemies,
detesting superstition.
Voltaire (1694-1778)

Dying is easier than writing a novel.
Italo Svevo (1861-1928)

By and by
God caught his eye.
David Mc Cord's epitaph on a waiter.

But O for the touch of a vanished hand,
and the sound of a voice that is still!
Alfred Lord Tennyson (1809-1992)

Cowards die many times before their deaths;
The valiant never taste death but once.
William Shakespeare (1564-1616)

I have never killed a man, but I have read many obituaries with great pleasure.
> *Clarence Darrow(1857-1938)*

A belief in hell and the knowledge that every ambition is doomed to frustration at the hands of a skeleton have never prevented the majority of human beings from behaving as though death were no more than an unfounded rumor, and survival a thing not beyond the bounds of possibility.
> *Aldous Huxley (1894-1963)*

We are miserable enough in this life, without the absurdity of speculating upon another.
> *Lord Byron (1788-1824)*

Maybe this world is another planet's hell.
> *Aldous Huxley (1894-1963)*

Hitherto man had to live with the idea of death as an individual; from now onward mankind will have to live with the idea of death as a species.
> *Arthur Koestler (1905-1983)*

The constant possibility that a human being may die at any moment means that every human being ought to live in each passing moment to the hilt, as if it were going to be the last.
> *Arnold Toynbee (1889-1975)*

Why should I fear death? If I am, death is not. If death is, I am not. Why should I fear that which cannot exist when I do?
> *Epicurus, (c.341-270 BCE)*

It is not death that a man should fear, but he should fear never beginning to live.
> *Marcus Aurelius (121-180)*

One cannot look directly at either the sun or death.
> *La Rochefoucauld (1613-1680)*

Biography lends to death a fresh horror.
> *Oscar Wilde (1854-1900)*

I didn't attend the funeral, but I sent a nice letter saying I approved of it.

> *Mark Twain (1835-1910)*

Because I could not stop for Death
He kindly stopped for me -
The carriage held but just ourselves
And immortality.
> *Emily Dickinson (1830-1886)*

Mortality weighs heavily on me like unwilling sleep.
> *John Keats (1791-1825)*

Why is it we rejoice at birth and grieve at a funeral? It is because we are not the person involved.
> *Mark Twain (1835-1910)*

The best way to get praise is to die.
> *Italian proverb*

People will forget what you said; people will forget what you did, but people will never forget what you made them feel.
> *Maya Angelou (1928-   )*

If, after I depart this vale, you ever remember me and have thought to please my ghost, forgive some sinner and wink your eye at some homely girl.
> *H. L. Mencken (1880-1956)*

The Latin word for love, "amor", can be interpreted as "a-mor", that is, not death.
> *Jacques de Beisieux*

You've got to have a dream. When you lose your dreams, you die. We have so many people walking around who are dead and don't even know it.

Despite their infinite powers, gods die with surprising frequency.
> *Leon Zeldis*

DEFINITION

To define something is to substitute the definition for the thing.
> *Georges Braque (1882-1963)*

The beginning of wisdom is the definition of terms.
> *Socrates (470?-399 BCE)*

To de-fine is to set down ends ("fine"). Therefore, God cannot be defined.
Leon Zeldis

DEMOCRACY

Democracy is based on the conviction that man has the moral and intellectual capacity, as well as the inalienable right , to govern himself with reason and justice.
Harry S. Truman (1884-1972)

The main difference between Greek and Hebrew myths lay in the fact that Greek myths were royal and aristocratic, while the Hebrew myths were democratic. In Greek myth, only the hero and his descendants, whatever their conduct, could expect a happy after-life, while men of lower status, however virtuous, were relegated to a dismal Tartarus. Among the later Jews, on the other hand, every righteous observer of the Mosaic Law, whatever his birth or station, was assured of the Heavenly Kingdom.
Robert Graves (1895-1985),

The people will always be so ignorant and weak, that it needs to be conducted by the small number of enlightened men.
Voltaire (1694-1778)
[Contrary to what many believe, Voltaire was not in favor of democracy. LZ]

Demagogy, ignorance and prejudice are the greatest vices or democracy, and the most difficult to be solved.
Condorcet (1745-1794).

The rights of men are reduced to the following four: personal security, free enjoyment of property, equality before the law, participation of the citizens in legislation.
Condorcet (1743-1794)

Democracy must be something more than two wolves and a sheep voting on what to have for dinner.
James Bovard

Under democracy one party always devotes its chief energies to trying to prove that the other party is unfit to rule – and both commonly succeed, and are right.
H. L. Mencken (1880-1956)

Democracy substitutes election by the incompetent many for appointment by the corrupt few.
>*George Bernard Shaw (1856-1950)*

As a rule, democracies have very confused or erroneous ideas on external affairs, and generally solve outside questions only for internal reasons.
>*Alexis de Tocqueville (1805-1859)*

The Democratic Party is like a mule - without pride of ancestry or hope of posterity.
>*Edmund Burke (1729-1797)*

The difference between a democracy and a people's democracy is the same as the difference between a jacket and a straitjacket.
>*Ronald Reagan (1911-2004)*

Let the people think they govern, and they will be governed.
>*William Penn (1644-1718)*

One man with courage makes a majority.
>*Thomas Jefferson (1743-1826)*

DEPRESSION

He's turned his life around. He used to be depressed and miserable. Now he's miserable and depressed.
>*David Frost (1939-   )*

There are no desperate situations; there are men who despair in certain situations.
>*La Bruyere (1645-1696)*

All of us are attending some funeral or other.
>*Charles Baudelaire (1821-1867)*

Depression is anger without the enthusiasm.

DEVIL

God and the devil are an effort at specialization and division of labor.
>*Samuel Butler (1835-1902)*

Satan hasn't a single salaried helper; the Opposition employs a million
>*Mark Twain (1835-1910)*

The devil can cite scripture for his purpose.
William Shakespeare (1564-1616)

The devil is the best gentleman of you all.
Daniel Defoe (1660-1731)

An apology for the Devil – it must be remembered that we have only heard one side of the case. God has written all the books.
Samuel Butler (1835-1902)

The devil is a gentleman who never goes where he is not welcome.
John A. Lincoln

It is so stupid of modern civilization to have given up believing in the devil when he is the only explanation of it.
Ronald Knox (1888-1957)

DIAMONDS

If all the facets in a diamond were cut parallel, the stone would have no life.

DICTIONARIES

It is often forgotten that dictionaries are artificial repositories, put together well after the languages they define. The roots of language are irrational and of a magical nature.
Jorge Luis Borges (1899-1986)

The circle of the English language has well-defined center but no discernible circumference.
James Murray (1837-1915), Editor of the Oxford English Dictionary

No dictionary of a living tongue can ever be perfect, since while it is hastening to publication, some words are budding and some falling away.
Samuel Johnson (1709-1784)

Completing the Oxford English Dictionary took seventy years of work; it had 15,490 pages of single-spaced text; 414,825 words; 1,827,306 illustrative quotations selected from over 5,000,000 quotations offered by a legion of volunteer readers.

DIET

I'm on a seafood diet: I see food and I eat it.
Steve Burns (1973-   )
Brain cells come and brain cells go, but fat cells live forever.

I am a nutritional overachiever.

DIPLOMACY

Above all, Gentlemen, no excessive zeal.
Talleyrand (1754-1838), Foreign Minister of France, addressing young diplomats before their first posting

Diplomacy is to do and say
the nastiest things in the nicest way.
Isaac Goldberg

An ambassador is an honest man sent abroad to lie for his country.
Sir Henry Wotton (1568-1639)

How is the world governed and how do wars begin? Diplomats tell lies to journalists and believe them when they see them in print.
Karl Kraus (1874-1936)

A diplomat is a man who always remembers a woman's birthday but never remembers her age.
Robert Frost (1874-1963)

A memorandum is written to protect the writer, not to inform his reader.
Dean Acheson (1893-1971)

Sincere diplomacy is no more possible than dry water or wooden iron.
Joseph Stalin (1879-1953)

Close alliances with despots are never safe for free states.
Demosthenes (385? - 322 BCE)

Appeasers believe that if you keep on throwing steaks to a tiger, the tiger will become a vegetarian.
Haywood Broun (1888-1939)

A diplomat is the man who, entering the bathroom and finding a naked woman, promptly retires saying: 'Excuse me, sir'.

Diplomacy is the art of saying "nice doggy" until you can find a rock.

DOGS

When a man's best friend is his dog, that dog has a problem.
Edward Abbey (1927-1989)

Dogs represent a $7-billion-a-year industry in the United States.
The Atlantic Monthly, *March 1960, p. 49*

There is no psychiatrist in the world like a puppy licking your face.
Ben Williams

Outside of a dog, a book is a man's best friend. Inside a dog, it's too dark to read.
Groucho Marx (1895-1977)

Women and cats will do as they please, and men and dogs should relax and get used to the idea.
Robert A. Heinlein (1907-1988)

Don't accept your dog's admiration as conclusive evidence that you are wonderful.
Ann Landers (1918-   )

Heaven goes by favors. If it went by merit, you would stay out and your dog would go in.
Mark Twain (1835-1910)

DRINKING

Once in my safari in Africa somebody forgot the corkscrew and for several days we had to live on nothing but food and water.
W. C. Fields (1880-1946)

Anybody who hates dogs and loves whiskey can't be all bad.
W. C. Fields (1880-1946)

Work is the curse of the drinking classes.
Oscar Wilde (1854-1900)

I love to have a martini
Two at the very most.
After three, I'm under the table
After four, I'm under the host.
>   *Dorothy Parker (1893-1967)*

Noel Coward's formula for a perfect dry martini: fill the glass with gin, then very gently whisper 'vermouth' over the surface.

DRIVING

In the 18th century, philosophers argued that the gentry, riding horseback, always kept to the left side of the road, to leave their sword arm free, while the farmers, leading their animals by a rope held in their right hand, and keeping the animal between themselves and the ditch, walked on the right-hand side. Thus, when they met, the farmer had to give way and move over to the left of the road in order to pass. Philosophers thought this was not right, because it was the farmer, the son of toil, who made the wherewithal for the gentry to have horses.
At the time of the French revolution, Robespierre declared that the Commune of Paris would follow the rule of the road of the peasant farmer, everyone walking on the right side of the road to show with whom they were allied, the peasants and not the gentry. When Napoleon became Emperor, he declared as one of his first laws that the rule of the road adopted by the peasant farmer would apply to all the land he controlled.

At the time of their independence, the Americans declared fraternity with their brothers in France and followed the same principle. As civil wars swept through Europe in the early 19th century, the same declarations of fraternity were made and now, countries which have had civil wars drive on the right side of the road. It was only in 1960 that Sweden changed over, because of its land boundary with its neighbor, Norway. In the 1970's, the British West African countries changed for the same reasons. The Mano river was the site of the first fixed crossing between Liberia and Sierra Leone. It was agreed, by the Mano convention, that Sierra Leone would change, otherwise what would happen when traffic from either end of the bridge met in the middle?

This is the grave of Mike O'Day
Who died maintaining his right of way.
His right was clear, his will was strong
But he's just as dead as if he'd been wrong.
>   *Inscription on a gravestone*

DUTY

Duty is too often what we demand from others.
>   *La Bruyere (1645-1696)*

I slept and dreamt that life was joy. I awoke and found that life was duty.
I worked and, behold, duty is joy.
>   *Rabindranath Tagore (1861-1941)*

EDUCATION

Educate the children and you won't have to punish the men.
>   *Pythagoras of Samos (d. 497 BCE)*

Long is the road to teaching by theories; brief and effective by examples.
>   *Lucius Anneus Seneca (4 BCE-65 CE)*

All men by nature desire to know.
>   *Aristotle (384-322 BCE)*

What sculpture is to a block of marble, education is to a human soul.
>   *Joseph Adison (1672-1719)*

Education is movable property.
>   *Sammy Smooha*
>   *[Israeli professor, explaining the Jew's obsession with education. LZ]*

If you think education is expensive, try ignorance.
>   *Derek Bok (1930-   )*

Do not protect your children from the difficulties of life; teach them rather
to overcome them.
>   *Louis Pasteur (1822-1895)*

Education is what survives when what has been learned has been
forgotten.
>   *B. F. Skinner (1904-1990)*

Education is not the filling of a pail, but the lighting of a fire.
>   *William Butler Yeats (1865-1939)*
>   *[paraphrasing Plutarch]*

A good education should leave much to be desired.
>   *Alan Gregg (1952-   )*

The Future is a race between Education and Catastrophe.
Thomas Henry Huxley (1825-1895)

Perhaps the most valuable result of all education is the ability to make yourself do the thing you have to do when it ought to be done, whether you like it or not; it is the first lesson that ought to be learned, and however early a man's training begins, it is probably the last lesson that he learns thoroughly.
Thomas Henry Huxley (1825-1895)

Better not teach the peasants how to read; someone has to plow the fields.
Voltaire (1694-1778)

Rewards and punishment are the lowest form of education.
Chuang-Tzu, philosopher (4ᵗʰ c. BCE)
Change does not necessarily assure progress, but progress implacably requires change. Education is essential to change, for education creates both new wants and the ability to satisfy them
Henry Steele Commager (1902-1998)

He who opens a school door, closes a prison.
Victor Hugo (1802-1885)

When a subject becomes totally obsolete we make it a required course.
Peter Drucker (1909-2005)

Native ability without education is like a tree without fruit.
Aristippus (435? -356? BCE)

Socrates gave no diplomas or degrees.
G. M. Trevelyan (1876-1962)

Education… has produced a vast population able to read but unable to distinguish what is worth reading.
G. M. Trevelyan (1876-1962)

An university is the place where society and the State allow the clearest conscience of the times to flourish.
Karl Jaspers (1883-1969)

Education is not preparation for life; education is life itself.
Attributed to John Dewey (1859-1952)

If you plan for one year, plant rice; for ten years, plant trees; for a hundred years, educate men.
Motto of Berea College, Berea, Kentucky, USA

The objectives of Education are: "To offer every individual of the human species the means to provide his needs, to ensure his well-being, to know and exercise his rights, to understand and fulfill his duties."

"To ensure to each the ability to perfect his industry, to capacitate him for social functions to which he may be called, to develop to the full extent the aptitudes he has received from nature, and thus to establish equality of fact among the citizens, and to give reality to the political equality recognized by law."
Marquis de Condorcet (1743-1794

Every means should be used to illustrate those citizens who could not complete their education, or who did not profit enough from it, offering them the facility to acquire at any age the knowledge that might be useful to them....
Marquis de Condorcet (1743-1794)

I thank God we have no free schools or printing, and I hope that we shall not have these for a hundred years. For learning has brought disobediences and heresy and sects into the world; and printing has divulged them and libels against the government. God keep us from both.
Sir William Berkeley (1605-1677)

The total number of professors in the six largest universities of Argentine is 3,935, while the National Lottery employs 4,183.
La Nación, Buenos Aires, 7 May 1989

The only essential ingredients of education are appetite and enthusiasm.
Sir Winston Churchill (1874-1965)

It has well been said that the highest aim in education is analogous to the highest aim in mathematics, namely, to obtain not *results* but *powers*, not particular solutions, but the means by which endless solutions may be wrought.
George Eliot (1819-1880)

Everyone thinks of changing humanity, but no one thinks of changing himself.
Leo Tolstoy (1828-1910)

A teacher should never use the word 'no' or any other negative locution, and in order to achieve this ideal, a teacher must never ask a student a question the student can't answer.
Dr. Frank Charles Laubach (1884-1970)

If the aborigine drafted an IQ test, all of Western civilization would presumably flunk it.
Stanley Marion Gam (1922-   )

A teacher affects eternity; he can never tell where his influence stops.
Henry Adams (1838-1918)

Education is democracy. Only the teachers will eliminate the demagogues, the thugs, the tramps; that's why the whole country must become a school.
Domingo Faustino Sarmiento (1811-1888)

Tyranny is bad not because it assassinates those who rebel, but because it domesticates those who could rebel; cutting some heads who think is not so serious as preventing in advance that heads think.
José Ingenieros (1877-1925)

Aristotle was asked how superior is an educated man to the one lacking education. He replied: "as the living are compared to the dead".
Diogenes Laertius (c. 150 BCE)

Education is the transmission of civilization.
Will (1885-1981) and Ariel Durant (1898-1981)

My idea of education is to unsettle the minds of the young and inflame their intellects.
Robert Maynard Hutchins (1899-1977)

An American university is an athletic institution in which classes are held for the feeble-minded.

College is a fountain of knowledge… and the students are there to drink.

No one should be allowed to play the violin until he has mastered it.

There are two major products to come out of Berkeley: LSD and UNIX. We don't believe this to be a coincidence.

Education is the highest form of charity.
Leon Zeldis

I attribute the failure of our educational systems to the lack of Pedagogues, who have mostly been replaced by parrots whose least concern is forming the character of their pupils.
Leon Zeldis

EGO

A narcissist is someone better looking than you are.
Gore Vidal (1925-   )
Don't be humble. You're not that great.
Golda Meir (1898-1978)

Egotism is nature's compensation for mediocrity.
L. A. Safian

He had a protractile ego.
Leon Zeldis

EGOISM

People seem to enjoy things more when they know a lot of other people have been left out of the pleasure.
Russell Baker (1925-   )

Egoism is a pervading sense of "each man for himself", increasing intolerance regarding the opinions of others, a frenetic struggle to achieve wealth or power or both, never mind how.
Leon Zeldis

ELDORADO

Sir Walter Ralegh's prophecy that Eldorado would be discovered in Guiana was so tempting that it almost persuaded the Pilgrim fathers to sail there instead of to Virginia.
Vanora Bennet

ENCOURAGEMENT

Flatter me, and I may not believe you. Criticize me, and I may not like you. Ignore me, and I may not forgive you. Encourage me, and I will not forget you.
William Arthur Ward (1921-1997)

The deepest principle of Human Nature is the craving to be appreciated.
William James (1842-1910)

Though no one can go back and make a new start, anyone can start from now and make a new ending.
Carl Bard (1907-1978)

Too often we underestimate the power of a touch, a smile, a kind word, a listening ear, an honest compliment, or the smallest act of caring, all of which have the potential to turn a life around.
Leo Buscaglia (1924-1998)

If at first you don't succeed, skydiving is not for you.

END OF THE WORLD

Don't expect too much from the end of the world.
Stanislaw Lem (1921-2006)

A bad smell of extinction follows *Homo Sapiens* around the world.
Ronald Wright (1948-   )

If civilization is to survive, it must live on the interest, not the capital of nature.
Ronald Wright (1948-   )

ENEMIES

Don't criticize your enemies, they may learn something.
Juan Goytisolo (1931-   )

Observe your enemies, for they are the first to find out your faults.
Antisthenes (444?-371? BCE)

Nobody ever forgets where he buried the hatchet.
Kin Hubbard (1868-1930)

Forgive your evemies, but never forget their names.
John. F. Kennedy (1917-1963)

One must forgive one's enemies, but not before they are hanged.
Heinrich Heines (1797-1856)

There is nothing so common as to imitate the practice of enemies and to use their weapons.
> *Voltaire (1694-1778)*

Believing that a weak enemy is not dangerous is believing that a spark cannot cause a fire.
> *Sadi (c.1184-?1292)*

A man cannot be too careful in the choice of his enemies.
> *Oscar Wilde (1854-1900)*

Impotent hatred is the most horrible of all emotions; one should hate nobody whom one cannot destroy.
> *Johann von Goethe (1749-1832)*

If an enemy offers you his hand, look well what he's holding in the other.
> *Leon Zeldis*

The flea would like nothing better than a painless bite.
> *Leon Zeldis*

ENGLAND

In England there are sixty different religions and only one sauce.
> *Francesco Caracciolo (1752-1799)*

If you want to eat well in England you have to eat breakfast three times a day.
> *Somerset Maugham (1874-1965)*

Englishman: a creature who thinks he is being virtuous when he is only being uncomfortable.
> *George Bernard Shaw (1856-1950)*

Continentals have a sex life, Englishmen have hot water bottles.
> *George Mikes (1912-1987)*

When it's three o'clock in New York, it's still 1938 in London.
> *Bette Midler (1945-)*

The civic virtues, good manners, ingrained personal habits of self-control and moderation, and the national mistrust of excess have all been jettisoned or destroyed. Violence, hysteria, meanness and vulgarity are surely among the leading traits of the prevailing English temper.
> *Richard Davenport Hines (1953-), writing in 2005*

64

To be born English is to win first prize in the lottery of life.
Cecil Rhodes (i853-1902)

ENGLISH

The circle of the English language has well-defined center but no discernible circumference.
James Murray (1837-1915), Editor of the Oxford English Dictionary.

ENNUI

Necessity is the constant scourge of the lower classes, ennui of the higher ones.
Arthur Schopenhauer (1788-1860)

ENTHUSIASM

I prefer the errors of enthusiasm to the indifference of wisdom.
Anatole France (1844-1924)

If you aren't fired with enthusiasm, you will be fired with enthusiasm.
Vince Lombardi (1913-1970), football trainer

Not everything that is more difficult is more meritorious.
Saint Thomas Aquinas (1225-1274?)

Nobody made a greater mistake than he who did nothing because he could only do a little.
Edmund Burke (1729-1797)

Whatever you can do or dream you can do, begin it. Boldness has genius, magic and power behind it. Do it now.
Johann von Goethe (1749-1832)

Surtout, Messieurs, point de zéle.
(Above all, Gentlemen, without escessive zeal)
Talleyrand (1754-1838), addressing young diplomats before their first posting

Many are stubborn in the pursuit of the path they have chosen, few in pursuit of the goal.
Nietzsche (1844-1900)

It is unfortunate, considering that enthusiasm moves the world, that so few enthusiasts can be trusted to speak the truth.
Arthur Balfour (1848-1930)

EQUALITY

Equality is an ethical and not a biological principle.
Ashley Montagu (1905-1999)

Most politicians proclaim their love of equality, but then insist on preferential treatment for themselves.
Leon Zeldis

ERROR

Errors, like straws, upon the surface flow;
He who would search for pearls must dive below.
John Dryden (1631-1700)

We most often go astray on a well-trodden and much-frequented road.
Lucius Annaeus Seneca (4 BCE – 65 CE)

I prefer the errors of enthusiasm to the indifference of wisdom.
Anatole France (1844-1924)

To err is human, to forgive supine.
S.J. Perelman (1904-1979)

The world always makes the assumption that the exposure of an error is identical with the discovery of truth - that the error and truth are simply opposite. They are nothing of the sort. What the world turns to, when it is cured on one error, is usually simply another error, and maybe one worse than the first one.
H. L. Mencken (1880-1956)

There is no error so monstrous that it fails to find defenders among the ablest men.
Lord John Dalberg Acton (1834-1902)

A man should never be ashamed to own that he has been in the wrong, which is but saying, in other words, that he is wiser today than he was yesterday.
Jonathan Swift (1667-1745)

Until he died, Columbus had no idea of the existence of any land north of Panama, and still clung to his conviction that the large continent that was becoming apparent south of the Caribean was, somehow, part of Asia.

Printer's axiom: you can have it fast, cheap or accurate. Pick two.

ETHICS see also **MORALITY**

Ethics cannot be formulated.
> *Ludwig Wittgenstein (1889-1951)*

Ethics does not treat of the world. Ethics must be a condition of the world, like logic.
> *Ludwig Wittgenstein (1889-1951)*

Men are not punished for their sins, but by them.
> *Elbert Hubbard (1856-1915)*

EVIL (see also **WORDS INTO ACTS**)

Evil is like an arrow. A person who unsheathes a sword can regret his intention and return it to its sheath. But the arrow cannot be retrieved. So, too, words of slander once uttered, a person has no control over them anymore.
> *Jewish sages*

Men never do evil so completely and cheerfully as when they do it from religious conviction.
> *Blaise Pascal (1623-1662)*

Lack of money is the root of all evil.
> *George Bernard Shaw (1856-1950)*

The worst danger for the future of humanity is in the good and the just; no matter how much evil the bad ones can do, the evil done by the good ones is the most damaging.
> *Nietzsche (1844-1900)*

There is only one good, that is knowledge; there is only one evil, that is ignorance.
> *Socrates (470?-399 BCE)*

Great men will never do great mischief but for some great end.
> *E. Burke (1729-1797)*

It is as hard for the good to suspect evil, as it is for the bad to suspect good.
> *Marcus Tullius Cicero (106-43 BCE)*

The man who has been tortured once stays tortured.
> *Jean Améry (1912-1978)*
> *[Auschwitz survivor. Committed suicide]*

The only thing necessary for the triumph of evil is for good men to do nothing.
> *Attributed to Edmund Burke (1729-1797)*

To discuss evil in a manner implying neutrality, is to sanction it.
> *Ayn Rand (1905-1982)*

Every man should view himself as equally balanced: half good and half evil. Likewise, he should see the entire world as half good and half evil. With a single good deed he will tip the scales for himself, and for the entire world, to the side of good.
> *Moses ben Maimon (Maimonides) (1135-1204)*

Apathy is the glove into which evil slips its hand.
> *Bodie Thoene*

Sufficient unto the day is the evil thereof – but there is also a night shift.

EXPERIENCE

To most men, experience is like the stern lights of a ship, which illumine only the track it has passed.
> *Samuel Taylor Coleridge (1772-1834)*

Caminante, no hay camino,
Se hace el camino al andar.
Caminante, no hay camino,
Sino estelas en la mar.

(Traveller, there is no road,
while walking the road is made.
Traveller, there is no road,
but wakes on the wide sea)
> *Antonio Machado (1875-1939)*

Experience enables you to recognize a mistake when you make it again.
> *Franklin P. Jones*

A proverb is a short sentence based on long experience.
> *Miguel de Cervantes (1547-1616)*

EXPLANATIONS

If you can't explain something to your grandmother, then you probably don't really understand it.
> *Albert Einstein (1879-1955)*

"For example" is not proof.
> *Yiddish proverb*

The truth, though interesting, is hardly relevant.

To explain comes from "ex-plicare", cutting the stone.

Too many explanations hide a lie.
> *Leon Zeldis*

FAITH see BELIEF

FAME

People seldom become famous for what they say until after they are famous for what they have done.
> *Cullen Hightower (1923-   )*

Pourvu que ça dure.
(Provided it lasts).
> *Letitia Bonaparte, mother of Napoleon, upon hearing his coronation as Emperor*

After I'm dead I'd rather have people ask why I have no monument than why I have one.
> *Cato the Elder (234-149 BCE)*

God will not look you over for medals, degrees or diplomas, but for scars.
> *Elbert Hubbard (1856-1915)*

Glory is to an old man like diamonds to an old woman: it adorns but gives not beauty.
> *Chateaubriand (1768-1848)*

The splendors of earthly fame are no more than a wind that soon changes direction.
> *Dante Alighieri (1265-1321)*

It is good to have fame, but safer to have money.
> *Seneca (4 BCE- 65 CE)*

The pyramids are a useless and idiotic display of royal wealth.
> *Pliny the Elder (23-79)*

Pliny is frequently consulted, rarely read.
> *Sorcha Carey (1943-   )*

Fame is something which must be won; honor is something which must not be lost.
> *Arthur Schopenhauer (1788-1860)*

Dignity does not consist in possessing honors, but in deserving them.
> *Aristotle (384-322 BCE)*

If you are looking for his monument, look around.
> *Marble slab with the name Christopher Wren inscribed on it, in St. Paul's Cathedral in London*

It is not in the power of any man to command success; but you have done more - you have deserved it.
> *General George Washington praising Benedict Arnold, after the nearly successful siege of Quebec.*
> *[Arnold later became the most famous traitor in American history]*

No one looks at the blazing sun; all do when it is eclipsed.
> *Baltasar Gracián (1601-1658)*

What do Rudolf Christoph Eucken and Carl Friedrich Georg Spitteler have in common? They won the Nobel Prize for Literature. What do Franz Kafka and Aldous Huxley have in common? They never did.
> *Leon Zeldis*

FAMILY
One would be in less danger
From the wiles of the stranger
If one's own kin and kith
Were more fun to be with.
> *Ogden Nash (1902-1971)*

The awe and dread with which the untutored savage contemplates his mother-in-law are among the most familiar facts of anthropology.
> *Sir James Fraser (1854-1941)*

No matter how many communes anybody invents, the family always creeps back.
> *Margaret Mead (1901-1978)*
> *[Exactly what happened to the Israeli Kibbutz. LZ]*

The hatred of relatives is the most violent.
> *Tacitus (55? – 118?)*

Be careful how you treat your childrem – they get to pick your nursing home.
> *Bumper sticker*

FAMOUS LAST WORDS

They couldn't hit an elephant at this dist....
> *General John Sidgwick, shortly before being shot through the eye by a Confederate soldier*

Take out the pin and count what?

This is the wire I have to cut.

Don't worry, I took all the bullets out of the gun.

If the parachute doesn't open by itself, I have this little cord.

What do you mean, don't look back?

What edge?

Barking dogs never bite.

He never bit me.

I'm sure your husband will understand.

I'm sure your wife will understand.

Pressing this key deletes only the last word.

If you don't approach it, the bear won't attack.

FANATICISM

Fanaticism is overcompensation of doubt.
Carl Gustav Jung (1875-1961)

From fanaticism to barbarism is only one step.
Denis Diderot (1713-1784)

Fanaticism is not an error, but a blind and stupid frenzy that reason can never accept.
Jean-Jacques Rousseau (1712-1778)

The introduction of religious passion into politics is the end of honest politics, and the introduction of politics into religion is the prostitution of true religion.
Lord Halisham (1907-2001)

Fanaticism consists in redoubling your effort when you have forgotten your aim.
George Santayana (1863-1952)

All isms are wasms.
Dwight Eisenhower (1890-1969)

Pope Pius VII (1800-1823) refused to allow gaslight and smallpox vaccination in the papal territories (that were quite extensive at the time).
Frederick Brown (1851-1941)

FEAR

Keep your fears to yourself, but share your courage with others.
Robert Louis Stevenson (1850-1894)

The soldier fears death, but the general fears the hour of judgment.
Napoleon Bonaparte (1769-1821)

Let us not look back in anger, nor forward in fear, but around in awareness.
James Thurber (1894-1961)

Fear is the price of religious hope.
Roy Porter (1946-2002)

The sword makers of Toledo used to say, that steel is stained only by fear.
Antonio de Lezama (1882-1971)

A man who has been in danger, when he comes out of it forgets his fears, and sometimes he forgets his promises.
Euripides (c. 495-406 BCE)

More dangers have deceived men than forced them.
Francis Bacon (1561-1626)

When rats abandon a sinking ship, where exactly do they think they're going?
Douglas Gauck

Courage is resistance to fear, mastery of fear - not absence of fear.
Mark Twain (1835-1910)

Americans are always eager to entertain conspiracy theories. They flourish in the artificially nourishing soil of academe, immune to scientific reasoning and logical discourse.
Mary Lefkowitz (1935-   )

Fear of:

Baldness	Peladophobia
Beautiful women	Venustaphobia
Beards	Pogonophobia
Dancing	Chorophobia
Dentists	Dentophobia
Getting wrinkles	Rhytiphobia
Marriage	Gamophobia
Wine	Oenophobia
Work	Ergasiophobia

FILMS see also **MOVIES**

Sometimes you have to lie. One often has to distort a thing to catch its true spirit.

> *Robert Flaherty (1884-1951), film director, who put a harpoon in the hands of the Eskimo hero of* Nanook of the North *(who actually used guns), and revived the custom of shark-hunt in* Man of Aran, *a custom dead for more than 100 years*

FLATTERY

Whenever you commend, add your reasons for doing so; it is this which distinguishes the approbation of a man of sense from the flattery of sycophants and admiration of fools.

> *Richard Steele (1672-1729)*

The number of flatterers and of envious men is the same.

> *Seneca (4 BCE- 65 CE)*

One catches more flies with a spoonful of honey than with twenty casks of vinegar.

> *Henry IV of France (1553-1610)*

Flattery is like chewing gum. Enjoy it but don't swallow it.

> *Hank Ketcham (1920-2001)*

Rare is the man who does not believe the flatterer, while claiming to despise him.

> *Leon Zeldis*

FLOWERS

Begonia is named for Michel Begon (1638-1710)
Camellia is named for Georg Josef Kamel (1661-1706)
Fuchsia is named for Leonard Fuchs (1501-1566)
Poinsettia is named for Joel R. Poinsett (1799-1851)

FOOD

A 500 kg bull produces 500 g of protein in 24 hours, while 500 kg of bacteria produce from 5 to 50 tons in the same time. Ten to one hundred times faster!

> *Magazine Litéraire N° 171-173, May 1981, p. 45*

Tell me what you eat, and I will tell you what you are.
  Brillat-Savarin (1755-1826), famous gourmet

Dinners have become a means of government, and the fates of nations are decided at a banquet.
  Brillat-Savarin(1755-1826)

The trouble with Italian food is that five or six days later you're hungry again.
  George Miller (1920-)

Oysters are wildly fertile, releasing 50 million eggs at a time when spawning.
  Mark Kurlansky (1948-)

Every husband is his wife's pig, he eats whatever she prepares.

FOOLS

The shlemiel falls on his back and bruises his nose.
  Yiddish proverb

A fool sees not the same tree that a wise man sees.
  William Blake (1757-1827)

Nobody did anything very foolish except for some strong principle.
  Viscount Melbourne (William Lamb) (1779-1848)

The man who lives free from folly is not so wise as he thinks.
  La Rochefoucauld (1613-1680)

Wise men talk because they have something to say; fools, because they have to say something.
  Plato (427-347 BCE)

The only thing worse than the babbling of fools is to hear your own voice among them.
  Michael Cochran

You can fool most of the people most of the time.
  P. T. Barnum (1810-1891)

You can fool some of the people all of the time, and those are the ones you have to concentrate on.
>   *Robert S. Strauss (1918-   )*

When the wise man points to the moon, the fool looks at the finger.
>   *Chinese proverb*

Never approach a bull from the front, a horse from the rear, or a fool from any direction.
>   *Cowboy saying*

A wise man gets more from his enemies than a fool from his friends.
>   *Baltasar Gracián (1601-1658)*

FORGETTING

They may forget what you said, but they will never forget how you made them feel.
>   *Carl W. Buechner*

Forgetting the past is a disease.
>   *Dulce Chacón (1964-2003)*

He had a photographic memory that was never developed.

Many forgive injuries, but none ever forgave contempt.

The past should be abandoned not because it is bad, but because it is dead.

FRANCE see FRENCHMEN

FREEDOM

It is harder to free a people from subjection, than to subjugate a free one.
>   *Montesquieu (1689-1755)*

There are times when freedom must be covered with a veil, like the statues of gods.
>   *Montequieu (1689-1755)*

The basic test of freedom is perhaps less in what we are free to do than in what we are free not to do.
>   *Eric Hoffer (1902-1983)*

Russian empire.. a slave society in which only one man (or woman) in all the Empire is ever actually free.
Marquis de Custine (1790-1857)

What is liberty without wisdom and without virtue? It is the greatest of all possible evils, for it is folly, vice, and madness, without tuition or restraint.
Edmund Burke (1729-1797)

Liberty is being free from the things we don't like in order to be slaves of the things we do like.
Ernest Benn (1875-1954)

There is no generalized idea of liberty, and it is hard to form one, since the liberty of a particular man is exercised only at the expense of other people's. Formerly liberty was called privilege; all things considered, that is perhaps its true name.
Remy de Gourmont (1858-1915)

Tyranny is always better organized than liberty.
Charles Peguy (1873-1914)

Order without liberty and liberty without order are equally destructive.
Theodore Roosevelt (1858-1919)

Who is free? The wise man who can dominate his passions.
Horace (65-8 BCE)

Only the well-informed man is really free.
Albert Pike (1809-1891)

Freedom is deserved only by he who knows how to conquer it each day.
Johann von Goethe (1749-1832)

Freedom is nothing else but a chance to be better.
Albert Camus (1913-1960)

Absolute freedom mocks at justice. Absolute justice denies freedom.
Albert Camus (1913-1960)

The difference between a slave and a citizen is that a slave is subject to his master and a citizen to the laws. It may happen that the master is very gentle and the laws very harsh; that changes nothing. Everything lies in the distance between caprice and rule.
Simone Weil (1909-1943)

Well, if crime fighter fight crime and fire fighter fight fire, what do freedom fighters fight? They never mention that part to us, do they?
> *George Carlin (1938-   )*

FREEMASONRY

Freemasonry is broad humanitarianism; treating life as a practical experience, not ignoring the pleasures of refreshment and entertainment. The *material* in Masonry is equal to the *spiritual*; it is moral but not dogmatic; it demands sanity rather than sanctity; it is tolerant but not supine; it seeks truth but does not define truth. It espouses liberty and the dignity of man but has no platform or propaganda. It believes in the nobility and usefulness of life; it is moderate, universal and so liberal as to permit each individual to form and express his own opinions.
> *Philip Dormer Stanhope, Earl of Chertefield (1694-1773)*

The traditional forms of Masonry are like heirlooms transmitted from generation to generation.
> *José Martí (1853-1895)*

Michelangelo, though of noble birth, insisted that he was just a *tagliapietra*, a stonemason.
> *Joseph Rykwert (1926-   )*

A mason is an initiate, in permanent search for *being* and not for *having*.
> *Dr. Santiago Richter*

The average mind is like a pool of water violently agitated by windstorms: storms of passion, of desires, of duties to be done, of a hundred demands upon one's time, of restless hurrying to-and-fro, of irritations, anxieties, worries, and a thousand other ills of the mind. Concentration is the cure.
> *Julian P. Johnson*
> *[That is exactly the reason for the Opening Ritual in a MasonicLodge, LZ]*

Let us pray, that come it may,
And come it will for a' that,
That man to man the whole world o'er
Shall brothers be for a' that.
> *Robert Burns (1759-1796)*

Freemasonry comes in as many flavors as ice-cream.
> *Leon Zeldis*

FREE-WILL

There is no free-will in geometry nor in astronomy.
August Comte (1798-1857)

Everything is in the hands of heaven except the fear of heaven.
Mishna, *Seder Brachot 33b*

I must believe that I have free will. Indeed, I have no choice.

FRENCHMEN

France has neither winter nor summer nor morals. Apart from these drawbacks it is a fine country. France has usually been governed by prostitutes.
Mark Twain (1835-1910)

A relatively small and eternally quarrelsome country in Western Europe, fountainhead of rationalist political manias, military impotent, historically inglorious during the past century, democratically bankrupt, Communist-infiltrated from top to bottom.
William F. Buckley Jr. (1925-2008)

The French probably invented the very notion of discretion. It's not that they feel that what you don't know won't hurt you; they feel that what you don't know won't hurt them. To the French lying is simply talking.
Fran Lebowitz (1950-   )

Malice and spite are the two characteristics of the French.
Chateaubriand, François René de (1768-1848)

In Paris they simply stared when I spoke to them in French; I never did succeed in making those idiots understand their own language.
Mark Twain (1835-1910)

As far as I am concerned, war always means failure.
Jacques Chirac (1932-   ), President of France, opposing the 2003 war against Iraq's dictator Saddam Hussein.
And then he got this reply:
As far as France is concerned, you're right.
Rush Limbaugh (1951-   )

Going to war without France is like going deer hunting without your accordion.
Norman Schwarzkopf (1934-)

If France wasn't responsible for the Holocaust it's only because the Germans thought of it first.
Richard Littlejohn, The Sun *(UK), 18.4.02*

At the end of the 18th century one half of the French did not speak French.
Eric Hobsbowm (1917-)

A Frenchman's imagination is always at the call of his senses.
William Hazlitt (1778-1830)

Marx said that the French do everything twice; the first as tragedy and the second as farce.

FRIENDS

A bit of perfume always clings to the hand that gives the rose.
Chinese proverb

Opposition is true friendship.
William Blake (1757-1827)

Associate yourself with men of good quality if you esteem your own reputation, for 'tis better to be alone than in bad company.
George Washington (1732-1799)

Friendship cannot live with ceremony, nor without civility.
Marquis of Halifax (1633-1695)

Don't boast that friendship authorizes you to say unpleasant things to your friends. The closer a relation is with a person, the more necessary tact and courtesy become.
Oliver W. Holmes (1809-1894)

Assumptions are the termites of relationships.
Henry Winkler (1945-)

Benevolence, which seldom stays to chuse
Lest pausing Prudence teach him to refuse,
Friendship, which once determin'd, never swerves,
Weighs ere it trusts, but weighs not ere it serves.
Ann Yearsley (1753-1806)

A friend in power is a friend lost.
Henry Adams (1838-1918)

A hundred friends is too little; one enemy, too much.
Tibetan proverb

We cherish our friends not for their ability to amuse us, but for our own to amuse them.
Evelyn Waugh (1903-1966)

I value the friend who for me finds time on his calendar, but I cherish the friend who for me does not consult his calendar.
Robert Brault (1938-   )

Ladies and gentlemen are permitted to have friends in the kennel, but not in the kitchen.
George Bernard Shaw (1856-1950)

You could read Kant by yourself, if you wanted to; but you must share a joke with someone else.
Robert Louis Stevenson (1850-1894)

Most people enjoy the inferiority of their best friends.
Earl of Chesterfield (1694-1773)

Friendship is the joy, the inexpressible comfort of feeling safe with a person, having neither to weigh thoughts or to measure words, but pouring all right out as they are, chaff and grain together, confident that a faithful friendly hand will take and sift them, keep what is woth keeping, and with a breath of comfort, blow the rest away.
George Eliot (1819-1880)

We read that we ought to forgive our enemies, but we do not read that we ought to forgive our friends.
Cosimo de Medici (1389-1464)

There are three sorts of friend that are beneficial, and three sorts that are harmful. Friendship with the upright, with the true-to-death and with those who have heard much is beneficial. Friendship with the obsequious, with those who are good at accommodating their principles or those who are clever is harmful.
Confucius (551-479 BCE)

A friend will come when called in the good times, and without being called in the bad ones.
>   *Cicero (106-43 BCE)*

To educate yourself for the feeling of gratitude means to take nothing for granted. Nothing that is done for you is a matter of course.
>   *Albert Schweitzer (1875-1965)*

Tell me who your friends are, and I'll tell you who you are.
>   *Spanish proverb*

A fool and his money are my best friends.

When a friend succeeds, a little part of us dies inside.

He's the kind of a guy who lights up a room just by flicking a switch.

The most important word a man wants to hear is his own name.

Love thy neighbor as yourself, but choose yor neighborhood.

A good friend knows your faults, but doesn't remind you of them.
>   *Leon Zeldis*

FRUGALITY

Frugality is not difficult for the poor.
>   *Chinese proverb*

An ox for a penny - and if you haven't a penny?
>   *Yiddish proverb*

I need little, and the little I need, I little need.
>   *St. Francis of Assisi (1182-1226)*

They say the Scots keep the Sabbath and everything else they can lay their hands on.
>   *Ossian Lang (1865-1945)*

FUNDAMENTALISM

In the summer of 1999, evolution was removed from the list of subjects required to be taught in the high-school biology classes in the entire state of Kansas.
> Times Literary Supplement, *18.2.2000, p. 9*

The mind of the bigot is like the pupil of the eye; the more light you pour upon it, the more it will contract.
> *Oliver Wendell Holmes (1809-1894)*

Puritanism: The haunting fear that someone, somewhere may be happy.
> *H. L. Mencken (1880-1956)*

GENERALS

Generals cannot be trusted with anything, not even with war.
> *Georges Clemenceau (1841-1929)*

I don't subscribe to the idea that any fool can become a general. Only the biggest of them do.

GENERATIONS

The grandson remembers what the son wants to forget.
> *Yiddish saying*

Gentility is what is left over from rich ancestors after the money is gone.
> *John Ciardi (1916-1986)*

GENIUS

It is a sad thing to think of, but there is no doubt that Genius lasts longer than Beauty.
> *Oscar Wilde (1854-1900)*

Men of genius are often dull and inert in society, as a blazing meteor when it descends to earth, is only a stone.
> *Henry Wadsworth Longfellow (1807-1882)*

There was never a genius without a touch of madness.
> *Aristotle (384-322 BCE)*
> *[Also attributed to Seneca]*

Genius is for the ordinary practical living appropriate to normal mental powers an ill endowment, and, like every abnormality, an impediment.
Arthur Schopenhauer (1788-1860)

The world ... is only beginning to see that the wealth of a nation consists more than anything else in the number of superior men that it harbors... Geniuses are ferments, and when they come together, as they have done in certain lands at certain times, the whole population seems to share in the higher energy which they awaken.
William James (1842-1910)

GEOMETRY

No entrance to the ungeometrical.
Plato's inscription over the door of his Academy in Athens

Nature itself invites us to be Geometricians.
Christian Huygens (1629-1695)

Geometry existed before Creation. It is co-ethernal with the Mind of God. Geometry supplied God with a Model for Creation. God is Geometry itself.
Johannes Kepler (1571-1630)

GERMANS

A German joke is no laughing matter.
Mark Twain (1835-1910)

Germans laugh three times at a joke; the first, when they hear it; the second, when it's explained to them, and the third when they finally think they got it.

GLASGOW

I did not believe, until I visited the wynds of Glasgow, that so large an amount of filth, crime, misery and disease existed in one spot in any civilized country.
Friedrich Engels (1820-1895), visiting the city in 1888.
[The city has evolved since into a cultural hub. LZ]

GLORY

The glory of persons must always be measured by the means used to achieve it.
 La Rochefoucauld (1613-1680)

GLUTTONY

Gluttony, like bulimia, is often a symptom of spiritual starvation.
 Leon Zeldis

GOD

God does not reveal Himself in the world.
 Wittgenstein (1889-1951)

I believe in God, only I spell it Nature.
 Frank Lloyd Wright (1867-1959)

To believe in God is impossible – not to believe in Him is absurd.
 Voltaire (1694-1778)

After 1927, it is possible for an intelligent man to believe in God.
 Sir Arthur Eddington (1882-1944), cosmologist, referring to that year's synthesis of quantum mechanics

I solved the problem. God exists. It is we that don't exist.
 Amado Nervo (1870-1919) (committed suicide)

I don't know if God exists, but it would be better for His reputation if He didn't.
 Jules Renard (1864-1910)

He seems to have an inordinate fondness for beetles.
 J. B. S. Haldane (1892-1964), on God

If the eye had no solar nature it could never perceive the sun; if the force pertaining to God did not live in us, how could we ever conceive the divine?
 Johann von Goethe (1749-1832)

Earthly things must be known to be loved; divine things must be loved to be known.
 Blaise Pascal (1623-1662)

God winds up our hourglass.
>   *Georg Christoph Lichtenberg (1742-1799)*

To stand on one leg and prove God's existence is a very different thing from going down on one's knees and thanking him.
>   *Sören Kierkegaard (1813-1865)*

If God lived on earth, people would break his windows.
>   *Yiddish proverb*

When we talk to God, we're praying. When God talked to us, we're schizophrenic.
>   *Lily Tomlin (1939-   )*

I don't think that he's evil, but the worst you can say about him is that basically he's an underachiever.
>   *Woody Allen (1935 -   )*

The world is proof that God is a committee.
>   *Bob Stokes*

If a triangle could speak, it would say that God is eminently triangular, while a circle would say that the divine nature is eminently circular.
>   *Baruch Spinoza (1632-1677)*

Geometry existed before Creation. It is co-ethernal with the Mind of God. Geometry supplied God with a Model for Creation. God is Geometry itself.
>   *Johannes Kepler (1571-1630)*

Most gods have the manners and morals of a spoiled child.
>   *Robert Heinlein (1907-1988)*

Even God cannot change the past.
>   *Agathon (447?-401 BCE)*
>   *[Wrong. God can change the past and at the same time change all our memories of the past, written or mental, as well as the results of that change. LZ]*

If the gods listened to the prayers of men, all humankind would quickly perish, since they constantly pray for many evils to befall one another.
>   *Epicurus (c. 341-270 BCE)*

The nature of God is a circle of which the center is everywhere and the circumference is nowhere.
Attributed to Empedocles (c.490-c.430 BCE)

Never has a god been buried, who later does not rise from the dead.
Leopold Ziegler (1881-1958)

Despite their infinite powers, gods die with surprising frequency.
Leon Zeldis

It is not the fact that the starry sky is beautiful that proves the existence of God, but the fact that we are capable of appreciating its beauty.
Leon Zeldis

To de-fine is to de-limit, to put limits. Therefore, God cannot be de-fined.
Leon Zeldis

Even a simple thing, like magnetism, can be observed only through its effects. How, then, can we pretend to know God, if not through His effects? (e.g. the fact that we are able to distinguish between good and evil).
Leon Zeldis

GOOD

There is only one good, that is knowledge; there is only one evil, that is ignorance.
Socrates (470?-399 BCE)

The beautiful is the symbol of the morally good.
ImmanuelKant (1724-1804)

There is nothing either good or bad but thinking makes it so.
William Shakespeare (1564-1616)

The opposite of good is good intentions.
Kurt Tucholsky (1890-1936)

He who would do good to another must do it in minute particulars; general good is the plea of the scoundrel, hypocrite and flatterer. For art and science cannot exist but in minutely organized particulars.
William Blake (1757-1827)

In Latin-derived languages, related words define beauty and good.
    Bello e buono, Belle et bon, Bello y bueno.
        Also in other languages:
    Latin: *pulcher* = good and beautiful
    Greek: *Kalos* = healthy, agreeable
    Kalos kai agathos = "beautiful and valiant"
    Egyptian: *nepher* = good and beautiful
    (hence: Nephertiti, Nephertari, etc.)
    Hebrew: *yafeh* = beautiful, also good.
    Leon Zeldis

There is no good or evil in nature. Good is only conceivable within the human social environment, beyond the individual, where he can practice the virtues of justice and charity... or do evil.
    Leon Zeldis

GRATITUDE

Men are never attached to you by favors.
    Napoleon Bonaparte (1769-1821)

Be silent as to services you have rendered, but speak of favors you have received.
    Lucius Annaeus Seneca (45 BCE – 65 CE)

To educate yourself for the feeling of gratitude means to take nothing for granted... Nothing that is done for you is a matter of course.
    Albert Schweitzer (1875-1965)

He who confers a favor should at once forget it.
    Demosthenes (385?-322? BCE)

I feel a very unusual sensation – if it is not indigestion, I think it must be gratitude.
    Benjamin Disraeli (1804-1881)

GOVERNMENT

Every country has the government it deserves.
    Joseph de Maistre (1753-1821)

Government is not reason; it is not eloquence; it is force! Like fire, it is a dangerous servant and a fearful master.
    George Washington (1723-1792)

The two enemies of the people are criminals and Government.
Thomas Jefferson (1743-1826)

Government's view of the economy could be summed up in a few short phrases: It if moves, tax it. If it keeps moving, regulate it. And if it stops moving, subsidize it.
Ronald W. Reagan (1911-2004)

The government is like a baby's alimentary canal, with a happy appetite at one end and no responsibility at the other.
Ronald W. Reagan (1911-2004)

Government does not solve problems, it subsidizes them.
Ronald W. Reagan (1911-2004)

All governments are obscure and invisible.
Francis Bacon (1561-1626)

When Government fears the people, it's liberty. When people fear the Government, it's tyranny.
Benjamin Franklin (1706-1790)

There is no trick to being a humorist when you have the whole government working for you.
Will Rogers (1879-1935)

As a rule, democracies have very confused or erroneous ideas on external affairs, and generally solve outside questions only for internal reasons.
Alexis de Tocqueville (1805-1859)

Onagrocracy – government by asses.
Benedetto Croce (1866-1952)

The Ten Commandments contain 297 words, the Bill of Rights 463 words, and Lincoln's Gettysburg Address 266 words. A recent federal directive regulating the price of cabbage contains 26,911 words.
An article in the New York Times

Let the people think they govern, and they will be governed.
William Penn (1644-1718)

Just as it is impossible to know when a swimming fish is drinking water, so it is impossible to find out when a government servant is stealing money.
>   *Kautilya, The Arthrashastra (Science of Wealth), c. 300 BCE*

A government that robs Peter to pay Paul can always depend on the support of Paul.
>   *George Bernard Shaw (1856-1950)*

Our task now is not to fix the blame for the past, but to fix the course for the future.
>   *John F. Kennedy (1917-1963)*

For every action there is an equal and opposite government program.

The beatings will continue until morale improves.
>   [*This appears to be the motto of most governments. LZ*]

GREATNESS

The price of greatness is responsibility.
>   *Winston Churchill (1874-1965)*

He is a great man who uses earthenware dishes as if they were silver; and he is equally great who uses silver as if it were earthenware.
>   *Seneca (4 BCE-65 CE)*

A man of undoubted genius, but genius for what precisely it would be remarkably difficult to say.
>   *T. S. Eliot (1888-1965), referring to Windham Lewis*

If you would stand well with a great mind, leave him with a favorable impression of yourself; if with a little mind, leave him with a favorable impression of himself.
>   *Samuel Taylor Coleridge, (1772-1834)*

The characteristic of a great man is his power to leave a lasting impression on people he meets.
>   *Winston Churchill (1874-1965)*

I studied the lives of great men and famous women, and I found that the men and women who got to the top were those who did the jobs they had in hand, with everything they had of energy and enthusiasm and hard work.
>   *Harry S. Truman (1884-1972)*

90

Although I know we have already grown accustomed to less beauty, less elegance, less excellence, yet perversely I have confidence in the opposite of egalitarianism; in the competence and excellence of the best among us. The urge for the best is an element of humankind as inherent as the heartbeat. It may be crushed temporarily but it cannot be eliminated. If incompetence does not kill us first, we will win. We will always have pride in accomplishment, the charm of fine things - and we will win horse races. As long as people exist, some will always strive for the best. And some will attain it.
Barbara Tuchman (1912-1989)

HABIT

Habit is a cable. We weave a thread of it every day until it becomes so strong we cannot break it.
Horace Mann (1796-1859)

Habit is the best servant, but the worst master.
Nathaniel Emmons (1745-1840)

The child is father of the man.
William Wordsworth (1770-1850)

HAPPINESS

Happiness will come only when all men are equal, but equality will come only when all men are perfect.
Joseph Ernest Renan (1823-1892)

There is a principle in nature, more universal even than what is called natural light, more uniform still for all men, present in the most stupid as in the brightest: the desire to be happy.
Pierre Maupertuis (1698-1759)

If you want to live a happy life, tie it to a goal, not to people or things.
Albert Einstein (1879-1955)

O, how bitter a thing is to look into happiness through another man's eyes.
William Shakespeare (1564-1616)

Don't look back on happiness, or dream of it in the future. You are only sure of today, do not let yourself be cheated out of it.
Henry Ward Beecher (1813-1887)

Pithagoras placed happiness in the contemplation of the rhythm of the Universe (literally: perfection directed by numbers).
Heraclitus (6th-5th c. BCE)

One of the keys to happiness is a bad memory.
Rita Mae Brown (1944-)

Some cause happiness wherever they go, others cause happiness whenever they go.
Oscar Wilde (1854-1900)

There are as many nights as days, and the one is just as long as the other in the year's course. Even a happy life cannot be without a measure of darkness, and the word 'happy' would lose its meaning if it were not balanced by sadness.
Carl Jung (1875-1961)

Good friends, good books and a sleepy conscience: that is the ideal life.
Mark Twain (1835-1910)

The pleasures of the intellect are permanent, the pleasures of the heart are transitory.
Henry David Thoreau (1817-1862)

A happy person is not a person in a certain set of circumstances, but rather a person with a certain set of attitudes.
Scottish proverb

A human being is not one in pursuit of happiness but rather in search of a reason to become happy.
Viktor E. Frankl (1905-1997).

Men are anxious to improve their circumstances, but are unwilling to improve themselves, they therefore remain bound.
James Allen (1864-1912)

We have no more right to consume happiness without producing it than to consume wealth without producing it.
George Bernard Shaw (1856-1950)

There is no greater sorrow than to recall, in misery, the time when we were happy.
Dante Alighieri (1265-1321)

Happiness is a by-product. You cannot pursue it by itself.
Sam Levenson (1911-1980)

Happiness is in the journey, not the destination.

I never knew real happiness until I got married, and then it was too late.

Happiness is in little things: a little mansion, a little yacht, a little fortune.

If money won't make you happy, you won't like poverty either.

Puritanism: the haunting fear that someone somewhere may be happy.

Can perfect happiness result from imperfect things? If the most exquisite perfume is put into a bottle that first contained vinegar, will it smell as sweet? Though we may have words of wisdom before us, can we appreciate them properly if our soul is sullied? If reason is tainted by passion, will it serve as a guide?
Leon Zeldis

HATRED

Impotent hatred is the most horrible of all emotions; one should hate nobody whom one cannot destroy.
Johann von Goethe (1749-1832)

Like the greatest virtue and the worst dogs, the fiercest hatred is silent.
Jean Paul Richter (1763-1825)

One does not hate so long as one despises.
Nietzsche (1844-1900)

Hate is not the opposite of love; apathy is.
Rollo Muy (1909-1994)

I never hated a man enough to give him his diamonds back.
Zsa Zsa Gabor (1917-   )

We have just enough religion to make us hate, but not enough to make us love one another.
Jonathan Swift (1667-1745)

HEALTH

Health is merely the slowest possible rate at which one can die.
Larry Stimmel (1944-   )

Health nuts are going to feel stupid some day, lying in hospital dying of nothing.
Redd Foxx (1922-1991)

As for me, except for an occasional heart attack, I feel as young as I ever did.
Robert Benchley (1889-1945)

The presence of words and dialogue in the practice of medicine point to pure original theatrical performance, directly related to religious ritual, where faith and hope are not excluded.
Marco Antonio de la Parra (1952-   )

It's no longer a question of staying healthy. It's a question of finding a sickness you like.
Jackie Mason (1931-   )

I'm on a seafood diet: I see food and I eat it.
Steve Burns (1973-   )

Every sickness is a musical problem, and every cure a musical solution.
Novalis (1772-1801)

I don't deserve this award, but I have arthritis and I don't deserve that either.
Jack Benny (1894-1974)

If you think health care is expensive now, wait until you see what it costs when it's free.
P. J. O'Rourke (1947-   )

I get my exercise acting as a pallbearer for my friends who exercise.
Chauncey Depew (1834-1928)

It has been proven scientifically that for each kilometer you jog you add one minute to your life, This gives you, when you reach 85 years of age, an additional five months to live ... under geriatric care at $10,000 per month.

Malaria ("bad air") got its name from the Italians (previously it was known as "ague"), who finally eradicated it only in 1962. The malaria parasite was discovered in 1880 by the French army doctor Alphonse Laveran, and the beneficial properties of quinine were known since the 17th century.

If swimming is good for the figure, how do you explain whales?

Men lose their health to make money, then use the money to recover health.

Bad thoughts are dangerous for your health.
Leon Zeldis

HEAVEN

The network of heaven has wide meshes, yet nothing escapes it.
Lao-Tsu (604?-531?)

Heaven, as conventionally conceived, is a place so inane, so dull, so useless, so miserable, that nobody has ever ventured to describe a whole day in heaven, though plenty of people have described a day at the seaside.
George Bernard Shaw (1856-1950)

If heaven is above and hell is below, what's in the middle? A mixture of both.
Leon Zeldis

HELL

If you are going through hell, keep going.
Winston Churchill (1874-1965)

Perhaps our world is the hell of another planet.

HEROISM

The heroic man does not pose; he leaves that for the man who wishes to be thought heroic.
Elbert Hubbard (1856-1915)

There are stars whose radiance is visible on earth though they have long been extinct. There are people whose brilliance continues to light the world though they are no longer among the living. These lights are particularly bright when the night is dark.
>*Hanna Senesh, Jewish patriot, killed by the Nazis while trying to assist the underground in Hungary during WW2*

Show me a hero and I will write you a tragedy.
>*F. Scott Fitzgerald (1896-1940)*

Show me a hero, and I'll show you a corpse.
>*Mario Puzo (1920-1999)*

HISTORY

All history is contemporary history.
>*R. G. Collingwood (1889-1943)*

Historian's Rule: Any event, once it has occurred, can be made to appear inevitable by a competent historian.
>*Lee Simonson (1888-1967)*

A historian is an unsuccessful novelist.
>*H. L. Mencken (1880-1956)*

History has the relation to truth that theology has to religion, i.e. none to speak of.
>*Robert Heinlein (1907-1988)*

At least in the short run, what happens matters less than what people think happens.
>*George Lukacs (1906-1987)*

A country losing touch with its own history is like an old man losing his glasses. A distressing sight, at once vulnerable, unsure and easily disoriented.
>*George Walden (1939-   )*

The nations which have put mankind most in their debt have been small states: Israel, Athens, Florence, Elizabethan England.
>*Dean William Inge (1860-1954)*

History is a kingdom of lies.
>*Juan Goytisolo (1931-   )*

God cannot alter the past. That is why He had to create so many historians.
Samuel Butler (1835-1902)

History is the essence of innumerable biographies.
Thomas Carlyle (1795-1881)

History is a self-flattering account written by the winners, while tradition is what the losers actually recall as having happened.
Walter Benjamin (1892-1940)

The concept of a Middle Age standing between the golden age of antiquity and the modern dates only from 1469.
Jack Lynch (1917-1999)

The age of chivalry is gone. That of sophisters, economists and calculators has succeeded; and the glory of Europe is extinguished forever.
Edmund Burke (1729-1797), on the French Revolution

Want of foresight, unwillingness to act when action would be simple and effective, lack of clear thinking, confusion of counsel until the emergency comes, until self-preservation strikes its jarring gong – these are the features which constitute the endless repetition of history.
Winston Churchill (1874-1965)

History will be kind to me for I intend to write it.
Winston Churchill (1874-1965)

The one duty we owe to history is to rewrite it.
Oscar Wilde (1854-1900)

History is a book that writes us as we write it.
Jorge Luis Borges (1899-1986)

History is bunk.
Henry Ford (1863-1947)

History is a set of lies agreed upon.
Napoleon Bonaparte (1769-1821)

History would be an excellent thing if only it were true.
Leo Tolstoy (1828-1910)

The past as such does not exist. Recovering it is an illusion which you can enjoy until you realize that what is considered the past recaptured is no more than a present state of mind or humor.
Martin Walser (1927-)

I like the dreams of the future better than the history of the past.
Thomas Jefferson (1743-1826)

The trouble with our times is that the future is not what it used to be.
Paul Valéry (1871-1945)
[cf. Nostalgia is not what it used to be]

Let us not go over the old ground, let us rather prepare for what is to come.
Cicero (106-43 BCE)

Incredulity is the foundation of history.
Voltaire (1694-1778)

In Jewish history, the road between being sick and dying is a very long one.
Isaac Bashevis Singer (1904-1991)
[He was probably thinking of the Yiddish language. LZ]

We know that research is the most important step in the study of history. Comprehensive and accurate information must be available for those who would interpret trends in world happenings. History is made by men. In the study of the past, we must know the motives that inspired men who made history. Events and dates are of no value unless we can discover what caused the events at the dates stated, in what passes for History.
Harry S. Truman (1884-1972)

What history teaches us is that men have never learned anything from it.
Georg W. Hegel (1770-1831)

Our ignorance of history makes us libel our own time. People have always been like this.
Gustave Flaubert (1821-1890)

What is important in history is not only the events that occur but the events that obstinately do not occur. The outstanding non-event of modern times was the failure of religious belief to disappear. Nietzsche, who had so accurately predicted the transmutation of faith into political zealotry and the will to power, failed to see that the religious spirit could, quite illogically, coexist with secularization and resuscitate the dying God.

In the eighteenth and still more in the nineteenth century, the Western elites were confident in the evolution of humanity towards a governance by reason. A prime discovery of modern times is that reason plays little part in our affairs. Even scientists are not moved by it. As Max Planck sorrowfully observed: 'A new scientific truth is not usually presented in a way to convince its opponents. Rather, they die off, and a rising generation is familiarized with the truth from the start'.

Schopenhauer said with humor that the mission of history is showing that things have always been the same, but at any moment differently: *eadem sed aliter*.
> *José Ortega Gasset (1883-1955)*

One of the lessons of history is that "nothing" is often a good thing to do and always a clever thing to say.
> *Will Durant (1885-1981)*

The grandson remembers what the son wants to forget.
> *Yiddish saying*

For the Greeks, the distinction between myth and history was only one of distance in time.
> *Christopher P. Jones*

The hottest places in hell are reserved for those who in times of great moral crisis maintained their neutrality.
> *Dante Alighieri (1265-1321)*

The past is altered by the present as much as the present is directed by the past.
> *T. S. Eliot (1888-1965)*

The tapestry of history has no point at which you can cut it and leave the design intelligible.
> *George Dix (1901-1952)*

There is properly no history, only biography.
> *Ralph Waldo Emerson (1803-1882)*

We all live in the past, because there is nothing else to live in. To live in the present is like proposing to sit on a pin. It is too minute... To live in the

future is a contradiction in terms. The future is dead, in the perfectly definite sense that it is not alive.
Gilbert Keith Chesterton (1874-1936)

Historians should study problems in preference to periods.

HOLOCAUST

I have seen all the pictures from Buchenwald – it's impossible to be a poet any longer.
Halldór Laxness (1902-1998)

All culture after Auschwitz – the radical critique of culture included – is rubbish.
Theodor W. Adorno (1903-1969)

HONESTY

The most honest people of the world are the French who think and the English who speak.
Charles de Saint-Evremond (1610-1703)

I can promise to be sincere, but not to be impartial.
Johann von Goethe (1749-1832)

The louder he talked of his honor, the faster we counted our spoons.
Ralph Waldo Emerson(1803-1882)

No one can earn a million dollars honestly.
William Jennings Bryan (1860-1925)

For the merchant, even honesty is a financial speculation.
Charles Baudelaire (1821-1867)

There is no well-defined boundary line between honesty and dishonesty. The frontiers of one blend with the outside limits of the other, and he who attempts to tread this dangerous ground may be sometimes in the one domain and sometimes in the other.
O. Henry (William Sidney Porter) (1862-1910)

I would rather be the man who bought the Brooklyn Bridge than the man who sold it.
Will Rogers (1879-1935)

We all wear masks, and the time comes when we cannot remove them without removing some of our own skin.
Andre Berthiaume

You can't cheat an honest man.
W.C. Fields (1880-1946)

Honest people are socially dysfunctional.

HOPE

We have lost the taste for prophesy, let's not lose the duty of hope.
Raymond Aron (1905-1983)

Although I know we have already grown accustomed to less beauty, less elegance, less excellence, yet perversely I have confidence in the opposite of egalitarianism; in the competence and excellence of the best among us. The urge for the best is an element of humankind as inherent as the heartbeat. It may be crushed temporarily but it cannot be eliminated. If incompetence does not kill us first, we will win. We will always have pride in accomplishment, the charm of fine things - and we will win horse races. As long as people exist, some will always strive for the best. And some will attain it.
Barbara Tuchman (1912-1989)

Hope is generally a wrong guide, though it is a very good companion by the way.
Marquis of Halifax (1633-1695)

Hope has a good memory, gratitude a bad one.
Baltasar Gracián (1601-1658)

Most of the important things in the world have been accomplished by people who have kept trying when there seemed to be no hope at all.
Dale Carnegie (1888-1955)

Hope springs eternal in the human breast.
Alexander Pope (1688-1744)

HUMANITY

Each human being is bred with a unique set of potential that yearns to be fulfilled as surely as the acorn yearns to become the oak within it.
Aristotle (384-322 BCE)

As human beings, we are continuously linked to universal life and the simple vibration of an insect's antennae reverberates in the infinities of the cosmos.
Amado Nervo (1870-1919)

I love humanity, what bugs me is people.
Susan, friend of Mafalda, a character invented by the Argentinean cartoonist Quino

Whoever kills a human being annihilates all humankind.
Elie Wiesel (1928-   )

It is human nature to think wisely and act foolishly.
Anatole France (1844-1924)

We are not human beings having a spiritual experience. We are spiritual beings having a human experience.
Teilhard de Chardin (1881-1955)

Till recently it was thought proper to pretend that hman beings are very much alike, but in fact anyone able to use his eyes knows that the average human behavior differs from contry to country. Things that could happen in one country could not happen in another.
George Orwell (1903-1950)

HUMOR

A person without a sense of humor is like a wagon without springs - jolted by every pebble in the road.
Henry Ward Beecher (1813-1887)

For health and the constant enjoyment of life, give me a keen and ever-present sense of humor; it is the next best thing to an abiding faith in providence.
George B. Cheever (1807-1890)

If you want to make people weep, you must weep yourself. If you want to make people laugh, your face must remain serious.
Giovanni Jacopo Casanova (1725-1798)

The total absence of humor from the Bible is one of the most singular things in all literature.
Alfred North Whitehead (1861-1947)

A rich man's joke is always funny.
    T.E. Brown (1830-1897)

The Window has four Little Panes;
    But one have I –
The Window Panes are in its Sash;
    I wonder why!
    Oliver Herford (1863-1935)

Why doesn't Tarzan have a beard?

Give me ambiguity or give me something else.

Honk if you like peace and quiet.

Save the whales. Collect the whole set.

If you are poor and want to be rich, you are ambitious; if you are rich and want to make some more money, you are a greedy bastard.
    Leon Zeldis

IGNORANCE

Beware of false knowledge; it is more dangerous than ignorance.
    George Bernard Shaw (1856-1950)

The standard of proof for truth is far higher than for ignorance and prejudice.
    John Day (1574-1640?)

Everybody is ignorant, only on different subjects.
    Will Rogers (1879-1935)

Everything unknown is heavenly.
    Tacitus (55?-118? CE)

The wise man always wants to learn; the ignorant one, to teach.
    Nina Yomerowska

If English was good enough for Jesus Christ, it's good enough for the children of Texas.
    Miriam "Ma" Ferguson (1875-1961), Governor of Texas, defending a law banning the teaching of foreign languages in Texas schools [Apparently she never heard of Hebrew, Aramaic and Greek. LZ].

He thought that an erector set belongs in a porno shop.

Ignorance can be fixed - stupid is forever.

Learning dies when one knows all.

Knowledge is limited; ignorance, on the other hand, is boundless.
    Leon Zeldis

ILLUSTRIOUS

Illustrious is all that illuminates, and illuminating glows.
    Dante (1265-1321)

IMAGINATION

Imagination is the power to produce images and the temptation to incarnate these images - it is part of human nature. Imagination: the faculty of our nature to change it self.
    Charles Baudelaire (1821-1867)

Imagination is more important than knowledge.
    Albert Einstein (1879-1955)

He who has imagination without learning has wings and no feet.
    Joseph Joubert (1754-1824)

The imaginary is as real as the material. The trace of a dream is no less real than that of a step or the furrow of a plow on the ground.
    Georges Duby (1919-1996)

The opportunities of man are limited only by his imagination; but so few have imagination that there are ten thousand fiddlers to one composer.
    Charles F. Kettering (1876-1958)

The right honorable gentleman is indebted to his memory for his jests, and to his imagination for his facts.
    R. B. Sheridan (1751-1816)

I had a monumental idea this morning but I didn't like it.
    Samuel Goldwyn (1882-1974)

Imagination is what sits with Mom and Dad the first time their teenager stays out late.

IMMORTALITY

Ants have lived for more than 80 million years, while man's civilization is scarcely more than 7000 years old. They are the oldest cosmopolites; they have sheltered longest, grown food, escaped many of the violences of the mammalian world. Have they changed? It would seem they have changed very little if at all. They are one of the small "immortals". They attained their present relatively high biological specialization very long ago and have since been marking time or evolving so slowly that the modifications are extremely small.
> *Loren C. Eiseley (1907-1977)*

Millions long for immortality who don't know what to do on a rainy Sunday afternoon.
> *Susan Ertz (1894-1985)*

INCOME

I'm living so far beyond my income that we may almost be said to be living apart.
> *e. e. cummings (1894-1962)*

Live within your income, even if you have to borrow to do so.
> *Josh Billings (1818-1885)*

INCOMPETENCE

Never ascribe to malice that which is adequately explained by incompetence.
> *Napoleon Bonaparte (1769-1821)*

Always acknowledge a fault frankly. This will throw those in authority off their guard and give you the opportunity to commit more.
> *Mark Twain (1835-1910)*

In a hierarchy every employee tends to rise to his level of incompetence.
> *Dr. Laurence J. Peter (1919-1990)*

Even if you are on the right track, you'll get run over if you just sit there.
> *Will Rogers (1879-1935)*

The first Rule of Holes is that when you are in one, you should stop digging. To keep right on doing what is already causing disastrous consequences is either insane or profoundly stupid.
> *Molly Ivins (1944-2007)*

He's a walking advertising for eugenics.

Vegetarian: Indian word for lousy hunter.

Impossible is what timidity forbids us.
  Leon Zeldis

INEFFABLE

There is in fact the ineffable; it is shown, not told; it's the mystic.
  Ludwig Wittgenstein (1889-1951)

Describe in words the perfume of a rose.

INGRATITUDE

When somebody receives something to which he's not entitled, he seldom gives thanks.
  Francisco de Quevedo (1580-1645)

How sharper than a serpent's tooth it is
to have a thankless child!
  William Shakespeare (1564-1616)

INHERITANCE

We have not inherited the land from our fathers, rather we took it on loan from our children.
  Massai tribesman

INJUSTICE

There may be times when we are powerless to prevent injustice, but there must never be a time when we fail to protest.
  Elie Wiesel (1928-   )

INSANITY

Insanity in individuals is something rare – but in groups, parties, nations and epochs, it is the rule.
  Friedrich Nietzsche (1844-1900)

INSULTS

Ugly words, even said lightly, offend.
Seneca (4 BCE- 65 CE)

A gentleman never insults someone unintentionally.
Oscar Wilde (1854-1900)

INTELLECTUALS

There are some ideas so stupid only an intellectual would believe them.
George Orwell (1903-1950)

Intellectual capital needs to be constantly reinvested; a strategy of pure expenditure soon exhausts one's credit.
Stefan Collini (1947 -   )

The trouble with intellectuals is that they are not necessarily intelligent.

INTELLIGENCE

Sometimes I think the best proof of the existence of intelligent life in the universe is that no one has tried to contact us.
Bill Watterson (1958-   )

So fas as I can remember, there is not one word in the Gospels in praise of intelligence.
Bertrand Russell (1872-1970)

There is nothing to irritating as somebody with less intelligence and more sense than we have.
Don Herold (1889-1966)
Artificial intelligence is no match for natural stupidity.

Everyone is entitled to be stupid, but some abuse the privilege.

Intelligence is circular. The super-intelligent and the super-idiot often join hands.
Leon Zeldis

INTROSPECTION

We dream of journeys through the universe. Is not the universe inside us? We do not know the depth of our spirit. The mysterious path leads within. Eternity is inside us or nowhere, the future and the past.
>*Novalis (1772-1801)*
>*[cf. the alchemical V.I.T.R.I.O.L., LZ]*

"Know thyself?" If I knew myself, I would run away.
>*Johann von Goethe (1749-1832)*

It is as hard to see one's self as to look backwards without turning around.
>*Henry David Thoreau (1817-1862)*

In his private heart no man much respects himself.
>*Mark Twain (1835-1910)*

INTUITION

Intuition is to thinking as observation is to perception.
>*Rudolph Steiner (1861-1925)*

INVENTION

Invention is the mother of necessity.
>*Thorstein Veblen (1857-1929)*

I never heard of anyone ever stumbling on something sitting down.
>*Charles Kettering (1876-1958)*

IRRATIONALITY

Irrationally held truths may be more harmful than reasoned errors.
>*Thomas H. Huxley (1825-1895)*

In 1897 the lower house of the Indiana State Legislature (USA) adopted (67 to 0) a resolution (Engrossed Bill 246) defining the mathematical ireational number Pi as the rational figure 3.2 – the ratio of 4 to 5/4. This "discovery" would be made available to all schools in Indiana. Fortunately, the upper house heard the opportune intervention of a mathematician, Prof. Clarence Waldo, who happened to be present when the bill was read, and was able to convince the honorable legislators that the proposal was nonsense.
>*Contributed by William S. Aronstein*

Madness takes its toll. Please have exact change.

JAPAN

The bonsai is the ultimate expression of a reductive mentality. It is still seen most strikingly in the stifling of individual creativity in the educational system.
  Ian Buruma (1951-   )

Japan is a country that runs hundreds of super-express trains on time every day, but is also one in which half the human habitations are not even connected to main sewers.

JEWS

The Roman siege of Jerusalem, which lasted five months, was the largest in the entire Imperial period, and involved enormous forces: four full legions, detachments of two others, twenty infantry cohorts, eight mounted regiments and 18,000 auxiliaries supplied by local rulers. This was a much bigger force than the one used to conquer Britain a quarter-century before.
  Fergus Millar.

In Israel, in order to be a realist you must believe in miracles.
  David Ben-Gurion (1886-1973)

I always regretted not being a Jew.
  Jorge Luis Borges (1899-1986)

Israel, the only country where parents learn their mother tongue from their children.
  Ephraim Kishon (1924-2005)

You should have children just like you.
  Jewish mother's curse

The remarkable thing about my mother is that for thirty years she served us nothing but leftovers. The original meal has never been found.
  Calvin Trillin (1935-   )

If a poor man eats a chicken, one of them is sick.
  Shalom Aleichem (1859-1916)

Jewish festivities in brief: They wanted to kill us, they couldn't, let's eat!

JOURNALISM

Journalism is a profession whose business is to explain to others what it personally does not understand.
> *Lord Northcliffe (1865-1922)*

I am unable to understand how a man of honor could take a newspaper in his hands without a shudder of disgust.
> *Charles Baudelaire (1821-1867)*

How is the world governed and how do wars begin? Diplomats tell lies to journalists and believe them when they see them in print.
> *Karl Kraus (1874-1936)*

The newspaper is the natural enemy of the book, as the whore is of the decent woman,
> *The Goncourt Brothers (1822-1896 and 1830-1870)*

The newspaper is the second hand in the clock of history; and it is not only made of baser metal than those which point to the minute and the hour, but it seldom goes right.
> *Schopenhauer (1788-1860)*

For those who govern, the first thing required is indifference to newspapers.
> *Louis Adolphe Thiers (1797-1877)*

I keep reading between the lies.
> *Goodman Ace (1899-1982)*

Study Finds Sex, Pregnancy Link
> Cornell Daily Sun, *7.12.1995*
> *[this certainly proves the value of college education. LZ]*

Journalists should warn: you have the right to remain silent. Anything you say will be misquoted, then used against you.

The journalist races to meet his deadline; the writer's deadline is his death.
> *Leon Zeldis*

Journalists: a pack of rats racing to nibble at the facts, but usually confusing the holes for the cheese.
Leon Zeldis

JUDGING

We judge ourselves by what we feel capable of doing, while others judge us by what we have already done.
Henry Wadsworth Longfellow (1807-1882)

We are all inclined to judge ourselves by our ideals; others by their acts.
Harold Nicolson (1886-1968)

To judge without understanding constitutes an offence against morality.
Clifford Geertz (1926-2006)

Judgment can be acquired only by acute observation, by actual experience in the school of life, by ceaseless alertness to learn from others, by study of the activities of men who have made notable marks, by striving to analyze the everyday play of causes and effects, by constant study of human nature.
B. C. Forbes (1880-1954)

In our judgment of human transactions, the law of optics is reversed, we see the most indistinctly the objects which are close around us.
Richard Whately (1787-1863)

JUSTICE

Comedy is justice.
Aristophanes (c. 456 - c. 386 BCE)

Without property there is no justice.
John Locke (1632-1704)

The Uniform Code of Military Justice is uniform, is a code and is military - and therefore has nothing to do with justice.
Charles Morgan Jr. (1930-   )

Absolute freedom mocks at justice. Absolute justice denies freedom.
Albert Camus (1913-1960)

Crime is contagious. If the government becomes a law-breaker, it breeds contempt for the law.

Justice Louis D. Brandeis (1856-1941)

There may be times when we are powerless to prevent injustice, but there must never be a time when we fail to protest.

Elie Wiesel, Nobel laureate (1928-   )

If you do bend the staff of justice, let it be not by the weight of gifts, but that of mercy.

Miguel de Cervantes (1547-1616)

Justice delayed is justice denied.

William E. Gladstone (1809-1898)

The vilest deeds like poison weeds
bloom well in prison-air;
it is only what is good in Man
that wastes and withers there.

Oscar Wilde (1854-1900)

According to Plato, to achieve Justice, men must first search for individual harmony, then harmony with those close to him, then with all people so that in the end, Complete Harmony will be achieved, Universal Harmony, which is Justice.

Justice is to God as beauty is to man.

Judge as you would like to be judged? Never! I want preferential treatment.

Leon Zeldis

KINDNESS

Too often we underestimate the power of a touch, a smile, a kind word, a listening ear, an honest compliment, or the smallest act of caring, all of which have the potential to turn a life around.

Leo Buscaglia (1924-1998)

One kind word can warm three winter months.

Japanese proverb

Wise sayings often fall on barren ground; but a kind word is never
thrown away.
Sir Arthus Helps (1813-1875)

Kindness is in our power, but fondness is not.
Dr. Samuel Johnson (1709-1784)

KINGS

With the guts of the last priest, let us strangle the last king.
Denis Diderot (1713-1784)

Looking for a democratic monarch in Europe is like trying to find an
atheist in heaven.
Joan Prim (1814-1870)

KISS

A kiss can be a comma, a question mark or an exclamation point.
Mistinguette (1875-1950)

KITSCH

Definition of kitsch: a Venus de Milo with a clock in its belly.
BBC Radio, quoted by Eric Wilson (1940-   )

Kitsch never goes out of style.

KNOWLEDGE

The next best thing to knowing something is knowing where to find it.
Samuel Johnson (1709-1784)

If you do now know the names of things, the knowledge of them is lost.
Carl Linnaeus (1707-1778)

Knowledge is alphabet soup, a puzzle with which you must build and
organize the reality of the cosmos.
Mario M. Pérez-Ruiz

All our knowledge begins with the senses, proceeds then to the
understanding, and ends with reason. There is nothing higher than
reason.
Immanuel Kant (1724-1804)

Wonder rather that doubt is the root of knowledge.
Abraham Joshua Heschel (1907-1972)

Learned men are the cisterns of knowledge, not the fountainheads.
James Northcote (1746-1831)

One's mind, once stretched by a new idea, never regains its original dimensions.
Oliver Wendell Holmes (1809-1894)

We can be knowledgeable with other men's knowledge, but we cannot be wise with other men's wisdom.
Michel de Montaigne (1533-1592)

When you know, you act; when you don't know, you teach or criticize.
George Bernard Shaw (1856-1950

Nobody shoud fear lack of knowledge. False knowledge is what must be feared. All the evil in the world is the result of it.
Leon Tolstoy (1828-1910)

We do not know a millionth of one percent about anything.
Thomas A. Edison (1847-1931)

Never try to tell everything you know. It may take too short a time.
Norman Ford

If a little knowledge is dangerous, where is a man who has so much as to be out of danger?
Thomas Henry Huxley (1825-1895)

The world is governed more by appearance than by realities, so that it is fully as necessary to seem to know something as it is to know it.
Daniel Webster (1782-1852)
[It makes you wonder about his dictionary. LZ]

Try to know everything of something, and something of everything.
Henry Peter, Lord Brougham (1778-1868)

If you want to know the past, look at the present which is its result. If you want to know the future, look at the present which is its cause.
Buddha (563?-453? BCE)

Amor est magis cognitivus quam cognitio.
(We know things better by love than by intellect)

In Sanscrit, knowledge is Vidya, from the root Vid, which also means to see.

KORAN

The first complete translation of the Koran into a European vernacular language was a French translation by André du Ryer, published in Paris in 1647.

LANGUAGE

Language is a system of signs that express ideas.
Ferdinand de Saussure (1857-1913)

Language is to intelligence like symbols to intuition.
Dion Fortune

Language is the mother, not the handmaid of thought.
Karl Kraus (1874-1936)

Language has always been the companion of empire.
Elio Antonio de Nebrija (1444-1522), author of the first Spanish grammar (1492) and the first Spanish dictionary (1495)

Hanging is too good for a man who makes puns; he should be drawn and quoted.
Fred Allen (1894-1956)

It's a strange model of language in which skating on thin ice can get you into hot water.
Franklin P. Jones

A language is never is a state of fixation, but is always changing; we are not looking as a lantern slide but at a moving picture.
Andrew Lloyd Jones

Language is the armory of the human mind; and at once contains the trophies of its past, and the weapons of its future conquests.
Samuel Taylor Coleridge (1772-1834)

Language of mass communication has turned words into fetishes for which men will fight and die.
> *Karl Kraus (1874-1936)*

It is in the word, in the saying that things come into being.
> *Martin Heidegger (1889-1976)*

The purpose of *Newspeak...* is to make all other modes of thought impossible.
> *George Orwell (1903-1950)*
> *[Like calling the most brutal dictatorships 'The Democratic Republic of...". LZ]*

Each word when used in a new context is a new word.
> *John Rupert Firth (1890-1960)*

Whoever controls the language, the images, controls the race.
> *Allen Ginsburg (1926-1997)*

The limits of my language mean the limits of my world.
> *Ludwig Wittgenstein (1889-1951)*

Language is a city to the building of which every human being brought a stone.
> *Ralph Waldo Emerson (1803-1882)*

It is often forgotten that dictionaries are artificial repositories, put together well after the languages they define. The roots of language are irrational and of a magical nature.
> *Jorge Luis Borges (1899-1986)*

The most important things are the hardest to say, because words diminish them.
> *Stephen King (1947-   )*

Of those who say nothing, few are silent.
> *Thomas Neill (1850-1892)*

The task of Anthropology is to research the unconscious mental structures that can be reached through institutions, or better in language.
> *Claude Levi-Strauss (1908-   )*

To see a painting is to hear it: understand what it says. Painting is also music, and above all language.
Octavio Paz (1914-1998)

A sublime and ineffable body of metaphysical truths is implicit in the structure of our language.
Wittgenstein (1889-1951)

All metaphysical doctrines are distortions of the structure of our language, projected on to the world. It is as if ripples on the surface of the water caused us to wonder why the objects under it have such curious shapes.
Ludwig Wittgenstein (1889-1951)

Art is the language of the beautiful.
Adolphe Pictet (1799-1875).

Charles V is said to have remarked that he spoke Spanish to God, French to men, Italian to women, and German (or Dutch) to his horse.
Theodore K. Rabb

Whenever the literary German dives into a sentence, that is the last you are going to see of him until he emerges on the others side of his Atlantic with his verb in his mouth.
Mark Twain (1835-1910)

Put in order the denominations. When denominations are incorrect, reasoning is incoherent.
Confucius (551-479 BCE)

'Philistinism' did not exist in the English of our day, perhaps because we have so much of the thing.
Mathew Arnold (1822-1888)

The English are polite by telling lies. The Americans are polite by telling the truth.
Malcolm Bradbury (1932-2000)

Perhaps the most significant feature of twentieth-century intellectual development has been the way in which the study of language has opened the route to an understanding of mankind, social history and the laws of how society functions.
Rosalind Coward

Spanish is Latin as spoken by the Basque.
    Miguel de Unamuno (1864-1936)

LAUGHTER

Man is the only animal that laughs and cries, because he is the only who understands the difference between what is and what should be.
    William Hazlitt (1778-1830)

One must destroy one's adversaries' seriousness with laughter, and their laughter with seriousness.
    Gorgias (483-378 BCE)

I hasten to laugh at everything for fear of having to weep.
    Beaumarchais (1732-1799), later used by Mariano de Larra, aka Figaro (1809-1837)

If you don't learn to laugh at trouble, you won't have anything to laugh at when you grow old.
    Ed Howe

It better befits a man to laugh at life than to lament over it.
    Seneca (4 BCE-65 CE)

One must have a heart of stone to read the death of Little Nell without laughing.
    Oscar Wilde (1854-1900)

The mind ought sometimes to be amused, that it may the better return to thought, and to itself.
    Phaedrus (5th century BCE)

LAWS

To retain respect for sausages and laws, one must not watch them in the making.
    Otto von Bismarck (1815-1898)

Laws are nothing without force.
    Napoleon Bonaparte (1769-1821)

Laws are like spiders' webs: if some poor weak creature comes up against them, it is caught; but a bigger one can break through and get away.
    Solon (c. 638 - c. 558 BCE)

The more laws and order are made prominent,
the more thieves and robbers there will be.
    Lao-Tzu (604?-531?)

Useless laws weaken the useful ones.
    Montesquieu (1689-1755)

Bad laws are the worst sort of tyranny.
    Edmund Burke (1729-1797)

Where law ends, there starts tyrany.
    John Locke (1632-1704)

How could a state be governed, or protected in its foreign relations if
every individual remained free to obey or not to obey the law according
to his private opinion?
    Thomas Hobbes (1588-1679)

A multitude of laws in a country, like a great number of physicians, is a
signal of weakness and malady.
    Voltaire (1694-1778)

The law, in its majestic equality, forbids the rich as well as the poor to
sleep under bridges.
    Anatole France (1844-1924)

It is criminal to steal a purse, daring to steal a fortune, a mark of greatness
to steal a crown. The blame diminishes as the guilt increases.
    Friedrich von Schiller (1759-1805)

Some circumstantial evidence is very strong, as when you find a trout in
the milk.
    Henry David Thoreau (1817-1862)

The people should fight for the law as for their city wall.
    Heraclitus (6th-5th c. BCE)

Lex dura, sed lex (the law is harsh, but that is the law)
    Latin saying

LAWYERS

We all know that the law is the most powerful of schools for the imagination. No poet ever interpreted nature as freely as a lawyer interprets the truth.
  Jean Giraudoux (1882-1944)

Reduce the number of lawyers. They are like beavers - they get in the middle of the stream and dam it up.
  Donald Rumsfeld (1932-   )

J.P. Morgan is reported to have said to his lawyers: I pay your huge fees not to tell me what I could do and what I couldn't do, but how to do what I want to do.

A scientist takes nothing for granted. A Minister takes everything on faith. A lawyer takes everything he can get.

It's reported that research laboratories are using lawyers instead of rats, the three main reasons being that lawyers are more plentiful, that lab assistants don't get attached to them, and that there are some things a rat will not do.

Advice to neophyte lawers: When the facts are against you, argue the law; when the law is against you, argue the facts; and when both are against you, scream and yell.

A doctor, an architect and a lawer discuss whose profession is older. The doctor claims his is, because God operated on Adam to make Eve; the architect objects, because before that God made the heavens and the earth: construction; the lawyer says no, before that was chaos. Who made chaos?

One lawyer in a town is poor. Two lawyers in a town are both rich.
Why vampires never suck the blood of lawyers? Professional courtesy.

And: Vampires are different from lawyers; they suck blood only at night.

LEADERSHIP

If you are riding ahead of the herd, take a look back every now and then to make sure it's still there.
  Will Rogers (1879-1935)

Leadership is action, not position.
　　Donald H. McGannon

LEARNING

It is by imitation far more than by precept that we learn everything, and what we learn thus, we acquire not only more effectually, but more pleasantly. This forms our manners, our opinions, our lives.
　　Edmund Burke (1729-1797)

Learning makes the wise wiser and the fool more foolish.
　　John Ray (1627-1705)

Studies serve for delight, for ornament, and for ability.
　　Francis Bacon (1561-1626)

There are three kinds of men. The ones that learn by reading. The few who learn by observation. The rest of them have to pee on the electric fence.
　　Will Rogers (1879-1935)

I have learned throughout my life as a composer chiefly through my mistakes and pursuit of false assumptions, not my exposure to founts of wisdom and knowledge.
　　Igor Stravinsky (1882-1971)

He who has imagination without learning has wings and no feet.
　　Joseph Joubert (1754-1824)

Learn as if you were to live forever, live as if you were to die tomorrow.
　　Latin saying

LEISURE

It is already possible to imagine a society in which the majority of the population, that is to say, the laborers, will have almost as much leisure as in earlier times was enjoyed by the aristocracy. When one recalls how aristocracies in the past actually behaved, the prospect is not cheerful.
　　W. H. Auden (1907-1973)

If God wanted me to touch my toes, He would have put them on my knees.

Whenever I have the feeling I should exercise I sit down until it passes.

LIES see **TRUTH**

LIFE

The more civilized a people is, the greater is its respect for life and the value given to human life.
>*Editorial,* Libertad Digital [Internet newspaper], *17.10.2003*

Our life has no end, just as our visual field has no end.
>*Ludwig Wittgenstein (1889-1951)*

That it will never come again
Is what makes life so sweet.
>*Emily Dickinson (1830-1886)*

When memories exceed dreams, the end is near.
>*Michael Hammer*

Life is a jest, and all things show it:
I thought so once, and now I know it.
>*John Gray, inscribed on his tomb.*

Life... is a tale told by an idiot, full of sound and fury, signifying nothing.
>*William Shakespeare (1564-1616)*

When we remember we are all mad, the mysteries disappear and life stands explained.
>*Mark Twain (1835-1910)*

Life is what happens while you are making other plans.
>*John Lennon (1940-1980) [cf. the next one]*

Life is not long, and too much of it must not pass in idle deliberation how it shall be spent.
>*Dr. Samuel Johnson (1709-1784)*

Too late for love, too late for joy
Too late, too late!
You loitered at the road too long
You trifled at the gate.
>*Christina Rosetti (1830-1894)*

The great majority of men are bundles of beginnings.
Ralph Waldo Emerson (1803-1882)

Many people die with their music still in them. Why is this so? Too often it is because they are always getting ready to live. Before they know it, time runs out.
Oliver Wendell Holmes, Jr. (1841-1935)

You can't do anything about the length of your life, but you can do something about its width and depth.
H. L. Mecken (1880-1956)

Life is like arriving late for a movie, having to figure out what was going on without bothering everybody with a lot of questions, and then being unexpectedly called away before finding out how it ends.
Joseph Campbell (1910-1971)

What is laid dow, ordered, factual, is never enough to embrace the whole truth; life always spills over the rim of every cup.
Boris Pasternak (1890-1960)

We think in generalities, but we live in detail.
Alfred North Whitehead (1861-1947)

Nowadays most men lead lives of noisy desperation.
James Thurber (1894-1961)

We must live in the world and make the most of it as we find it.
Michel de Montaigne (1533-1592)

If I were to wish for anything, I should not wish for wealth and power, but for the passionate sense of the potential, for the eye which, ever young and ardent, sees the possible. Pleasure disappoints, possibility never. And what wine is so sparkling, what so fragrant, what so intoxicating, as possibility!
Soren Kierkegaard (1813-1855)

Life is not something waiting for you, it is happening in you.
Sozen (1797-1868)

There are three ingredients to the good life: learning, earning and yearning.
Christopher Morley (1890-1957)

Dying is one thing, not living is another.
Louis Calaferte (1928-1994)

Life is Death. Organisms live because it parts are always dying.
Claude Bernard (1813-1878)

The fragment of a life, however typical, is not the sample of an even web.
George Eliot (1819-1880)

It is only possible to live happily ever after on a day to day basis.
Margaret Bonnano

Life is like painting a picture, not like adding a sum.
Oliver Wendel Holmes (1809-1894)

The meaning of life differs from man to man, from day to day and from hour to hour.
Viktor E. Frankl (1905-1997)

It is easy to stop when going up, but difficult when going down.
Napoleon Bonaparte (1769-1821)

Human life can only be understood as a constant striving after values.
Alfred North Whitehead (1861-1947)

The human condition is such that pain and effort are not just symptoms which can be removed without changing life itself, they are the modes in which life itself, together with the necessity to which it is bound, makes itself felt. For mortals, the "easy life of the gods" would be a lifeless life.
Hannah Arendt (1906-1975)

I slept and dreamed that life was beauty;
I woke, and found that life was duty.
Ellen S. Hooper

There is no short cut to life. To the end of our days, life is a lesson imperfectly learned.
Harrison Salisbury (1908-1993)

Life is the only game in which the object of the game is to learn the rules.
Ashley Brilliant (1933-)

About the time one learns how to make the most of life, the most of it is gone.
The Akron Beacon Journal

One learns in life to keep silent and draw one's own confusions.
Cornelia Otis Skinner (1901-1979)

Life offers two great gifts: time, and the ability to choose how to spend it. Planning is a process of choosing among those many options. If we do not choose to plan, then we choose to have others plan for us.
Richard I. Winword

This is the highest wisdom that I own... freedom and life are earned by those alone who conquer them each day anew.
Johann von Goethe (1749-1832)

Life is not lost by dying; life is lost minute by minute, day by dragging day, in all the thousand small uncaring ways.
Stephen Vincent Benet (1898-1943)

Life can only be understood backwards, but it must be lived forwards.
Soren Kierkegaard (1813-1855)

The art of living is more similar to a fight than to a dance.
Marcus Aurelius (121-180)

Do not commit the error, common among the young, of assuming that if you cannot save the whole of manking you have failed.
Jan de Hartog (1914-2002)

Our life is frittered away by detail. Simplify, simplify !
Henry David Thoreau (1817-1862)

Be conscious that you live to die, in order to turn from the temporal to the eternal.
Sigmund Freud (1856-1939)

Life is like playing the violin in public and learning the instrument as one goes on.
Samuel Butler (1835-1902)

It is a funny thing about life; if you refuse to accept anything but the best, you very often get it.
W. Somerset Maugham (1874-1965)

In three words I can sum up everything I've learned about life: it goes on.
Robert Frost, poet (1874-1963)

Security is mostly a superstition. It does not exist in nature... Life is either a daring adventure or nothing.
  Helen Keller (1880-1968)

All life is an argument about matters of taste.
  Nietzsche (1844-1900)

We do not live, but think ourselves.
  Jean Rimbaud (1854-1891)
  [cf. the next one]

By your thoughts you are daily, even hourly, building your life. You are carving your destiny.
  Ruth Barrick Golden

And how am I to face the odds
Of man's bedevilment and God's?
I, a stranger and afraid
In a world I never made.
  A. E. Housman (1859-1936)

It must be borne in mind that the tragedy of life does not lie in not reaching your goals; the tragedy of life lies in not having any goals to reach.
  Benjamin I. Mays

As a tale, so it life. Not how long it is, but how good it is, is what matters.
  Seneca (4 BCE-65 CE)

There is no wealth but life.
  John Ruskin (1819-1900)

We seem to live more in the model we create of the world rather than in the world itself.
  Michael Faulkner (1897-1962)

The secret of life is honesty and fair dealing. If you can fake that, you've got it made.
  Groucho Marx (1895-1977)

The deeper we look into nature, the more we recognize that it is full of life, and the more profoundly we know that all life is a secret and that we are united with all life that is in nature. Man can no longer live his life for

himself alone. We realize that all life is valuable and that we are united to all this life. From this knowledge comes our spiritual relationship to the universe.
    Albert Schweitzer (1875-1965)

Life is to be lived, not controlled, and humanity is won by continuing to play in the face of certain defeat.
    Ralph Ellison (1914-1994)

Life is a grindstone, and whether it grinds a man down or polishes him up depends on the stuff he's made of.
    Josh Billings (1818-1885)

All the world's a stage and most of us are desperately unrehearsed.
    Sean O'Casey (1880-1964)

The first half of our life is ruined by our parents, and the second half by our children.
    Clarence Darrow (1857-1938)

Life is a progress from want to want, not from enjoyment to enjoyment.
    Samuel Johnson (1709-1784)

As I grow to understand life less and less, I learn to live it more and more.
    Jules Renard (1864-1910)

What is life? It is the flash of a firefly in the night. It is the breath of a buffalo in the wintertime.
    Crowfoot, Native American warrior and orator (1821-1890).
    [Did he read Ecclesiastes in Hebrew? The Hebrew word "hevel" wrongly translated as "vanity" actually means just that: the vapor of breath in the cold air. LZ]

Life cannot give you joy
Unless you really will it.
Life just gives you time and space,
it's up to you to fill it.

Life has a big IF in the middle.

Life is like a roll of toilet paper. The closer it gets to the end, the faster it goes.

All of the animals except man know that the principal business of life is to enjoy it.

Thinking of the future, people forget the present; they live as if they will never die, and die without having ever lived.

Is not the biggest whoever fills the most space, but whoever leaves the greatest void.

Some days you are the dog; some days you are the hydrant.

LIGHT

A principal feature of light is its ability to banish any form of darkness. Put simply, a darkened auditorium must respond to the light of a single candle. But no matter how much more darkness one adds – say, by enlarging the auditorium – no amount of darkness can snuff out the light.
        Rabbi Yehuda Berg

I saw Eternity the other night
Like a great ring of pure and endless light.
        Henry Vaughan (1621-1695)

A candle loses nothing by lighting another candle.

LITERACY

The ratio of literacy to illiteracy is constant, but nowadays the illiterate can read and write.
        Alberto Moravia (1907-1990)

LITERATURE

In criticism, the only method is to be intelligent.
        T. S. Eliot (1888-1965)

Remarks are not literature.
        Gertrude Stein (1874-1946)

Post-modern prose is… a footnote that doesn't know when to stop.
        Dale Peck (1967-   )

Never trust the artist. Trust the tale. The proper function of a critic is to save the tale from the artist who created it.
        D. H. Lawrence (1885-1930)

Art makes visible the nature of things.
> *Rudolph Arnheim (1904-2007)*
> *[Could be applied to Literature. LZ]*

The American way is to seduce a man by bribery and make a prostitute of him. Or else to ignore him, starve him into submission and make a hack out of him.
> *Henry Miller (1891-1980)*

Mega biblion, mega kakon.
Greek saying: Big book, big mistake.

LODGING

I thank your highness for kindly continuing to take care of my nourishment, but I beg you to no longer take care of my lodging.
> *Voltaire (1694-1778), while jailed by the Duke of Orleans*

LOGIC AND SCIENCE

There was a young lady named Bright
Whose speed was faster than light;
She went out one day
In a relative way,
And returned the previous night.
> *Jean Harrowven*

Three years after the General Theory of Relativity was verified by Eddington, ending the belief in fixed space and time, Ludwig Wittgenstein, one of the key figures of the period, published his *Tractatus Logico-Philosophicus*, which cumulatively over the decades destroyed confidence in systematic philosophy as a guide to human reason.

If a Greek says all Greeks are liars, our logic is inadequate.
> *Leon Zeldis*

LONDON

There is nothing more terrible than the streets of London.
> *Montesquieu (1689-1755)*

I think that Paris is a beautiful city with the ugliest things, while London is an ugly city with very beautiful things.
> *Montesquieu (1689-1755)*

Hell is a city much like London.
>   *Percy Bysshe Shelley (1792-1822)*

In 1903, there were only three motor taxis in London, but 11,000 horse-drawn cabs, each equine dropping 7.5 tons of manure per annum.
>   *Trevor Fishlock,* Conquerors of Time
>   *[a calculation shows the annual amount of horse droppings reached 82,500 tons. God bless the automobile. LZ]*

LOVE

If all the sacred writings are holy, the Song of Songs is the holy of holies.
>   *Rabbi Akiva (50?-132 CE)*

No woman ever falls in love with a man unless she has a better opinion of him than he deserves.
>   *Ed Howe*

How can yu love your neighbor if you are incapable of loving yourself.
>   *Swami Kurmarajadasa (1973-   )*

The desire of the man is for the woman, but the desire of the woman is for the desire of the man.
>   *Madame de Stael (1766-1817)*

True love is like ghosts, which everybody talks about and few have seen.
>   *Francois, Duc de La Rochefoucauld (1613-1680)*

To love is not to look one at another, but to look both in the same direction.
>   *Antoine de Saint-Exupéry (1900-1944)*

When women love us, they forgive everything, even our crimes; when they do not love us, they give us credit for nothing, not even our virtues.
>   *Honoré de Balzac (1799-1850)*

He who is in love with himself has at least this advantage - he won't encounter many rivals in his love.
>   *Georg Christoph Lichtenberg (1742-1799)*

It is easier to love humanity as a whole than to love one's neighbor.
>   *Eric Hoffer (1902-1983)*

Love is more pleasant than matrimony for the same reason that novels are more entertaining than history.
Chamfort (Nicolas Sebastien-Roch) (1741-1794)

The difference between a passion and a fancy is that the fancy lasts longer.
Sydney Smith (1771-1845)

If you never want to see a man again, say "I love you. I want to marry you. I want to have children". They leave skid marks.
Rita Rudner (1956-   )

The lunatic, the lover and the poet
Are of imagination all compact.
William Shakespeare (1564-1616)

Love is like an hourglass, with the heart filling up as the brain empties.
Jules Renard (1864-1910)

When my love swears that she is made of truth,
I do believe her, though I know she lies.
William Shakespeare (1654-1616)

Love is the word used to label sexual excitement of the young, the habituation of the middle-aged, and the mutual dependence of the old.
John Ciardi (1916-1986)

The golden fleece of self-love is proof against cudgel blows but not against pinpricks.
Friedrich Nietzsche (1844-1900)

I have a strong feeling that the opposite of love is not hate, but apathy.
Leo Buscaglia (1924-1998)

I like not only to be loved, but to be told that I am loved; the realm of silence is long enough beyond the grave.
George Eliot (Mary Ann Evans) (1819-1880)

I love you not for who you are, but for who I am when I am with you.
Gabriel García Márquez (1928-   )

To be trusted is a greater compliment than to be loved.
George MacDonald (1824-1905)

Love is the eyes' magnet.
Ramón Llull (1235-1316)

A kiss is a lovely trick designed by nature to stop speech when words become superfluous.
Ingrid Bergman (1915-1982)

Love is an ideal thing, marriage a real thing; a confusion of the real with the ideal never goes unpunished.
Johann von Goethe (1749-1832)

Non clamor, sed amor.
Henry Wadsworth Longfellow's bookplate

The Latin word for love, "amor", can be interpreted as "a-mor", that is, not death.
Jacques de Beisieux
[Through love we achieve immortality. LZ]

Let the love-lorn lover cure insomnia
By murmuring AMOR VINCIT OMNIA.
Ogden Nash (1902-1971)

Love, as it is practiced in society, is merely the exchange of two momentary desires and the contact of two skins.
Sébastien Roch Nicolas – Chamfort (1741-1794)

How brief is love, how long forgetting.
Pablo Neruda (1904-1973)

Love is not a worn out periodical feeling, but a marvelous beginning repeated again and again.
Leon Zeldis

Like fire, love requires continuous stoking.
Leon Zeldis

LUCK

Some folks want their luck buttered.
Thomas Hardy (1840-1928)

The harder I work, the luckier I am.

Please God, let me prove to you that winning the lottery won't corrupt me.

Why don't we ever see the headline "Psychic wins Lottery"?

Good luck is what happens to others. Just reward is what happens to us.
Leon Zeldis

LUST

Familiarity breeds attempt.
Goodman Ace (1899-1962)

I have an intense desire to return to the womb. Anybody's.
Woody Allen (1935-)

What men desire is a virgin who is a whore.
Edward Dahlberg (1900-1977)

MALAPROPISMS

The cup of Ireland's miseries has been overflowing for centuries, and is not yet full.
Sir Boyle Roche (1743-1807)

Don't confuse me with the facts after I made up my mind.
Samuel Goldwyn (1882-1974)

This makes me so sore it gets my dandruff up.
Samuel Goldwyn (1882-1974)

I resent insinuendoes.
Mayor Richard J. Daley (1902-1976)

In this business you either sink or swim or you don't.
David Smith (1906-1965)

Outside of the killings, Washington has one of the lowest crime rates in the country.
Attributed to Marion Barry (1936-), Mayor of Washington

There is a lot of uncertainty that's not clear in my mind.
Atributed to Gib Lewis (1936-), Texas House Speaker

Everybody line up alphabetically according to your height.
Attributed to Casey Stengel (1891-1975)

That lowdown scoundrel deserves to be kicked to death by a jackass, and I'm just the one to do it.
A congressional candidate in Texas

The only thing to prevent what's past is to put a stop to it before it happens.

Mr. Speaker, how could I be in two places at once unless I were a bird?

Half the lies our opponents tell about us are untrue.

Why should we be concerned about posterity? What has posterity done for us?

I undertake to tread the narrow line between impartiality on the one hand and partiality on the other.

All along the untrodden paths of the future I can see the footprints of an unseen hand.

It's no exaggeration to say that the undecideds could go one way or another.

We must take the bull by the tail and look the situation in the face.
Dog for sale: eats anything and is fond of children.

MAN

Man is the measure of all things.
Pythagoras (d. 497 BCE)

In man, the things which are not measurable are more important than those which are measurable.
Alexis Carrel (1873-1944)

Man is a reasoning rather than a reasonable animal.
Alexander Hamilton (1757-1804)

Man is a king when he dreams, and a beggar when he reflects.
Friedrich Hölderlin (1770-1843)

Man is an animal suspended in webs of significance he himself has spun.
Max Weber (1864-1920)

Few men are of one plain, decided color; most are mixed, shaded and blended, and vary as much, from different situations as changeable silks do from different lights.
Lord Chesterfield (1694-1773)

A man is only what he knows.
Francis Bacon (1561-1626)

Man is nothing else than what he makes himself to be.
Jean-Paul Sartre (1905-1980)

Style is the man himself.
Georges Buffon (1707-1788)

I believe the best definition of man is the ungrateful biped.
Fedor Dostoevski (1821-1881)

Man – a creature made at the end of a week's work when God was tired.
Mark Twain (1835-1910)

Man is more important than men. God made man and not men in His image.
André Gide (1869-1951)

Man is the only animal that blushes. Or needs to.
Mark Twain (1835-1910)

Man is the only animal that laughs and weeps, for he is the only animal that is struck by the difference between what things are and what they might have been.
William Hazzlit (1778-1830)

Man – a being in search of meaning.
Plato (427? – 347 BCE)

Man – the featherless biped.

Man, the only animal with regrets.
Leon Zeldis

MANAGEMENT

Management by objectives works if you know the objectives. Ninety percent of the time you don't
> *Peter Drucker (1909-2005)*

Accomplishing the impossible means only that the boss will add it to your regular duties.
> *Doug Larson (1902-1981)*

The golden rule of management: find someone you can trust he'll make mistakes, then appoint him as your junior assistant.
> *Leon Zeldis*

MARRIAGE

To keep your marriage brimming
With love in the loving cup,
Whenever you're wrong, admit it;
Whenever you are right - shut up.
> *Ogden Nash (1902-1971)*

A little incompatibility is the spice of life, as long as he has income and she is pattable.
> *Ogden Nash (1902-1971)*

A good marriage would be between a blind wife and a deaf husband.
> *Michel de Montaigne (1533-1592)*
> *[Also attributed to many other writers]*

Keep your eyes wide open before marriage, and half shut afterwards.
> *Benjamin Franklin (1706-1790)*

A man may be a fool and not know it, but not if he is married.
> *H. L. Mencken (1880-1956)*

A husband is what is left of a man after the nerve is extracted.
> *Helen Rowland (1875-1950)*

My mother buried three husbands, and two of them were just napping.
> *Rita Rudner (1956-   )*

Brides are not happy, they are just triumphant.
> *John Barrymore (1882-1942)*

All marriages are mixed marriages.
  Chantal Saperstein

Since it has been unable to eliminate love, the Church has at least disinfected it, instituting marriage.
  Charles Baudelaire (1821-1867)

Where there is marriage without love, there will be love without marriage.
  Benjamin Franklin (1706-1790)

Marriage is an adventure – like going to war.
  G. K. Chesterton (1874-1936)

Marriage is the only adventure open to the cowardly.
  Voltaire (1694-1778)

Marriage: a book of which the first chapter is written in poetry and the remaining chapters in prose.
  Beverly Nichols

Politics doesn't make strange bedfellows – marriage does.
  Groucho Marx (1890-1977)

So heavy is the chain of wedlock that it needs two to carry it, and sometimes three.
  Alexandre Dumas (1802-1870)

Woman inspires us to great things, and prevents us from achieving them.
  Alexandre Dumas, fils (1824-1895)

Zsa Zsa Gabor is an expert housekeeper. Every time she gets divorced she keeps the house.
  Henry Youngman (1906-1998)

If you are afraid of loneliness, don't marry.
  Anton Chekhov (1860-1904)

Bigamy is having one wife too many. Monogamy is the same.
  Oscar Wilde (1854-1900)

The majority of husbands remind me of an orangutan trying to play the violin.
  Honoré de Balzac (1799-1850)

To marry a second time represents the triumph of hope over experience.
>   *Dr. Samuel Johnson (1709-1784)*

A man in love is incomplete until he has married. Then he's finished.
>   *Zsa Zsa Gabor (1917-   )*

By all means, marry. If you get a good wife, you will be very happy; if you get a bad one, you will become a philosopher.
>   *Socrates (470?-399 BCE)*

If I ever marry it will be on a sudden impulse, as a man shoots himself.
>   *H.L. Mencken (1880-1956)*

I married beneath me. All women do.
>   *Nancy, Lady Astor (1879-1964)*

Marriage is a great institution, but I'm not ready for an institution, yet.
>   *Mae West (1892?-1980)*

Any married man should forget his mistakes; there is no use in two people remembering the same thing.

A man needs a mistress... just to break the monogamy.

Marriage is not a word but a sentence.

Celibacy is not hereditary.

Marriages work better with a bad memory.
>   *Leon Zeldis*

MARTYRS

Martyrdom has always been a proof of the intensity, never of the correctness of a belief.
>   *Arthur Schnitzler (1862-1931)*

The tyrant dies and his rule is over; the martyr dies and his rule begins.
>   *Soren Kierkegaard (1813-1865)*

They who do not know how to live must make a merit of dying.
>   *George Bernard Shaw (1856-1950)*

Martyrdom is one of nature's natural selection processes.
> *Leon Zeldis*

MASONRY see FREEMASONRY

MATHEMATICS

It has well been said that the highest aim in education is analogous to the highest aim in mathematics, namely, to obtain not *results* but *powers*, not particular solutions, but the means by which endless solutions may be wrought.
> *George Eliot (1819-1880)*

Nature speaks mathematics.
> *Galileo Galilei (1564-1642)*

The numerator goes on the top!
> *Albert Einstein (1879-1955)*

Not everything that can be counted counts, and not everything that counts can be counted,
> *Albert Einstein (1979-1955)*

There is a deep-lying congruence between the mathematical and the aesthetic.
> *George Steiner (1929-   )*

The traveling salesman problem: find the shortest circuit for a salesman visiting various towns in his territory. The problem is simple to calculate for a small number of towns; for ten, say, there are a few hundred thousand possible circuits, but for twenty towns the possible circuits reach 200 thousand billion; for thirty towns the calculation is beyond the capabilities of existing computers, and for for fifty, the number of computational steps would exceed the number of electrons in the universe.
> *Brian Rotman*

The greatest equation, according to the readers of Physics World magazine, is Euler's Equation, which combines rational and irrational numbers to get zero.
> *Kenneth Chang*
> *[Euler's Equation: e to the power of i times Pi, plus 1, equals zero]*

Logarithms were invented by John Napier in 1614. The slide rule was invented eight years later by William Oughtred.

A polar bear is a rectangular bear after a coordinate transform.

Grabel's Law: 2 is not equal to 3 – not even for very large values of 2.

MEANING

The meaning of the universe is outside the universe.
> *Wittgenstein (1889-1951),* Tractatus

You'll never really know what I mean and I'll never know exactly what you mean.
> *Mike Nichols (1931-   )*

I can never be certain of what you will understand. As one Master forbidding his students from taking even the simplest written notes said, 'What I know is one thing; what I am able to put into words is another thing; what you hear is something else; and what you understand is something altogether different.'
> *William S. Aronstein*

No one means all he says, and yet very few say all they mean, for words are slippery and thought is viscous.
> *Henry Brooks Adams (1838-1918)*

The medium is the message because it is the medium that shapes and controls the shape and form of human associations and action.
> *Marshall McLuhan (1911-1981)*

MEANS TO AN END

The end is in the beginning.
> *Ralph Ellison (1914-1994)*
> *[cf. The child is father of the man]*

Keep a diary and one day it will keep you.
> *Mae West (1892-1980)*

Efficiency is doing things right. Effectiveness is doing the right thing.
> *Peter Drucker (1907-2005)*

All bad things have this in common, that they take the means for the end.

The future is rooted in the past.

MEDICINE see also **PHYSICIANS**

Taking clinical studies too seriously may be hazardous to your health.
Gerald Grob (1958-   )

A hospital is no place to be sick.
Samuel Goldwyn (1882-1974)

A virus is bad news wrapped in protein.
P.D. Medawar

General Anesthesia was discovered in 1846. Sir William Osler remarked that it was a miracle quite unanticipated in the Bible.

Does the name Pavlov ring a bell?

METAPHYSICS

I am much tempted to say of metaphysicians what Scaliger said of the Basques: 'They are said to understand one another, but I don't believe a word of it.'
Sébastien Chamfort (1741-1794)

To see a world in a grain of sand,
And a heaven in a wild flower,
Hold infinity in the palm of your hand,
An eternity in an hour.
William Blake (1757-1827)

It is the center hole that makes the wheel useful. Shape clay into a vessel. It is the space within that gives it worth.
Lao-Tzu (604?-531?)

MILITARY

The Uniform Code of Military Justice is uniform, is a code and is military - and therefore has nothing to do with justice.
Charles Morgan Jr.

Military justice is to justice what military music is to music.
Groucho Marx (1895-1977)

An army of stags led by a lion is more to be feared than an army of lions
led by a stag.
Chabrias (d. 357 BCE ?)

In 1799 General Tamax received a proposal from Napoleon, who wished
to enter the Russian service, but they were unable to agree, as Napoleon
demanded the rank of major.
Leo Tolstoy (1828-1910)

Napoleon was asked, 'Who do you consider to be the greatest generals?'
He responded saying, 'The victors.'
Donald Rumsfeld (1932-   )

There are three classes of intelligence: human intelligence, animal
intelligence, and military intelligence.
Aldous Huxley (1894-1963)

We trained hard and, just when it appeared that we were prevailing, we
were reorganized. What a wonderful method to give the illusion of
progress, whilst totally demoralizing the troops.
Seneca (4 BCE-65 CE)

The highest rank in the Israeli army is Mom.

MIRACLE

What is a miracle? The natural law of a unique event.
Eugen Rosenstock-Huessy

Miracles happen all the time. We are just blind and don't recognize them
for what they are.
Leon Zeldis

MISANTHROPE

Any man aged forty who is not a misanthrope has never loved mankind.
Chamfort (1741-1794)

I love mankind. It's the people I can't stand.
Charles Schultz (1922-2000)

MISTAKES

Half of our mistakes in life arise from feeling when we ought to think, and thinking when we ought to feel.
John Churton Collins

When I make a mistake, it's a beaut.
Fiorello La Guardia (1882-1947)

There are no mistakes, save one: the failure to learn from a mistake.
Robert Fripp (1946-)

The six most drastic mistakes made by us humans:
1.   The delusion that individual advancement is made by crushing others.
2.   The tendency to worry about things that cannot be changed.
3.   Insisting that a thing is impossible because we cannot do it ourselves.
4.   Refusing to set aside trivial preferences.
5.   Neglecting development and refinement of the mind, and not acquiring the habits of reading and study.
6.   Attempting to compel others to believe and live as we do.
Marcus Tullius Cicero (106-43 BCE)

We learn wisdom from failure much more than from success. We often discover what will do by finding out what will not do, and probably he who never made a mistake never made a discovery.
Samuel Smiles (1812-1904)

If you can't be a good example, then you'll just have to be a horrible warning.
Catherine Aird (1930-)

A life spent making mistakes is not only more honorable but more useful than a life spent doing nothing.
George Bernard Shaw (1856-1950)

Experience is the name everybody gives to his mistakes.
Oscar Wilde (1854-1900)

The 50-50-90 rule: Anytime you have a 50-50 chance of getting something right, there's a 90% probability you'll get it wrong.

MODERATION

Truly decent people only exist among men with definite convictions, whether conservative or radical; so-called moderates are much drawn to rewards, orders, commissions, promotions.
>*Anton Chekhov (1860-1904)*

MONEY

Lack of money is the root of all evil.
>*George Bernard Shaw (1856-1950)*

Money is like the fertilizer used on the ground: it's useless if you don't spread it.
>*Francis Bacon (1561-1626)*

Make money, money, honestly if you can,
If not, by any means at all, make money.
>*Quintus Horatius Flaccus (Horace) (65-8 BCE)*

Money may buy the husk of many things, but not the kernel. It brings you food, but not appetite; medicine, but not health; acquaintances, but not friends; servants, but not faithfulness; days of joy, but not peace or happiness.
>*Henrik Ibsen (1828-1906)*

Never invest your money in anything that eats or needs repairing.
>*Billy Rose (1899-1966)*

I have enough money to last me the rest of my life unless I buy something.
>*Jackie Mason (1931-   )*

MORALITY

What is morality in any given time or place? It is what the majority then and there happen to like, and immorality is what they dislike.
>*Alfred North Whitehead (1861-1947)*

The only good is knowledge, and the only evil is ignorance.
>*Socrates (470?-399 BCE)*

Times are bad. Children no longer obey their parents and everyone is writing a book.
>*Marcus Tullius Cicero (106-43 BCE)*

Avarice and luxury, those pests which have ever been the ruin of every great state.
> *Titus Livius Livy (59 BCE – 17)*

If a man once indulges himself in murder, very soon he comes to think little of robbing; and from robbing he comes next to drinking Sabbath-breaking, and from that to incivility and procrastination.
> *Thomas De Quincey (1785-1859))*

Like Leporello, learned men keep a list, but the point is what they lack; while Don Juan seduces girls and enjoys himself, Leporello notes down the time, the place, and a description of the girl.
> *Kierkegaard (1813-1865)*

If all the girls who attended the Yale prom were laid end to end, I wouldn't be a bit surprised.
> *Dorothy Parker (1893-1967)*

Moral certainty is always a sign of cultural inferiority. The more uncivilized the man, the surer he is that he knows precisely what is right and what is wrong. The truly civilized man is always skeptical and tolerant, in this field as in all others. His culture is based on "I am not too sure".
> *H. L. Mencken (1880-1956)*

Whenever morality is based on theology, whenever right is made dependent on divine authority, the most immoral, unjust, infamous things can be justified and established.
> *Ludwig Feuerbach (1804-1872)*

The most successful tempters and thus the most dangerous are the deluded deluders.
> *George C. Lichtenberg (1742-1799)*

I can try to be improper, but I may need some instruction.
> *Louise de la Vallière (1644-1710), about to become the mistress of king Louis XIV of France*

Moral indignation is jealousy with a halo.
> *H. G. Wells (1866-1946)*

We have, in fact, two kinds of morality side by side: one which we preach but do not practice, and another which we practice but seldom preach.
> *Bertrand Russell (1872-1970)*

Nature, in her indifference, makes no distinction between good and evil.
  Anatole France (1844-1924)

A corporation cannot blush.
  Ascribed to Howel Walsh (c. 1820)

All bad precedents begin as justifiable measures.

The beatings will continue until morale improves.

MOVIES

The producer is not a necessary evil...He's unnecessary, and he's an evil.
  Orson Welles (1915-1985)

Film-making consists of inventing impossible problems for yourself and then failing to solve them.
  John Boorman (1933-   ), English film director

Hollywood: a place where the inmates are in charge of the asylum.
  Laurence Stallings (1894-1968)

Sometimes you have to lie. One often has to distort a thing to catch its true spirit.
  Robert Flaherty (1884-1951), film director, who put a harpoon in the hands of the Eskimo hero of 'Nanook of the North' (who actually used guns), and revived the custom of shark-hunt in 'Man of Aran', a custom dead for more than 100 years

The first projector of moving pictures was presented by the Lumiére brothers on 22 March, 1895. The first film was 16 meters long. The first public performance took place on December 28, and the take was 32 francs.

Cinema is an industry of imbeciles, by imbeciles, for imbeciles.
  Leon Zeldis (with excuses to Abraham Lincoln)

Nothing is wrong with movies that a few millions less could not cure.
  Leon Zeldis

Hollywood's real name is Holloweed.
  Leon Zeldis

146

MUSIC

I know that the twelve notes in each octave and the variety of rhythm offer me opportunities that all of human genious will never exhaust.
Igor Stravinsky (1882-1971)

I have begun a lecture series on "Aesthetics and the Theory of Composition". As you can imagine, the object is to overturn both.
Arnold Schoenberg (1874-1951)

His music is not chaotic enough to be modern.
Theodor W. Adorno (1903-1969)

Is Wagner actually a man? Is he not rather a disease? Everything he touches falls ill. He has made music sick.
Friedrich Nietzsche (1844-1900)

Only sick music makes money today.
Friedrich Nietzsche (1844-1900)

Rhythm is to time as symmetry is to space.
Francis Warrain

The beginning of art is not reason.
Edgard Varèse (1883-1965)

The unconscious meaning of music corresponds to the unconscious meaning of life.
Franco Fornari (1921-1985)

To see a painting is to hear it: understand what it says. Painting is also music, and above all language.
Octavio Paz (1914-1998)

Music is a language without a dictionary, whose symbols are interpreted by the listener according to some unspoken Esperanto of the emotions.
Aaron Copland (1900-1990)

Music is the only sensual pleasure without vice.
Samuel Johnson (1709-1784)

My idea is renewing Music through its most intimate alliance with Poetry.
Franz Liszt (1811-1886)

Music is the one art form which works directly on the individual's feelings and not via the medium of thought.
>*Schopenhauer (1788-1860)*
>*[and the same could be said of some symbols. LZ]*

If only I could have gone to Italy, I might have become a first-rate opera composer.
>*Joseph Haydn (1732-1809)*
>*[In fact, he wrote about a dozen Italian operas for the Esterház stage, very well received. LZ]*

How wonderful opera would be if there were no singers.
>*Gioacchino Rossini (1792-1868)*

Wagner had some wonderful moments but awful half hours.
>*Gioacchino Rossini (1792-1868)*

The claque is absolutely necessary, not only for the artists, but because some operas are so boring that nobody would clap if we didn't boost up the atmosphere.
>*Antonio Carrara, organizer of the claque at La Scala of Milan*

Every day I am reborn and every day I must begin again.
>*Pablo Casals (1876-1973)*

Without music life would be a mistake.
>*Friedrich Nietzsche (1844-1900)*

Bach opens a vista to the universe. After experiencing him, people feel there is meaning in life after all.
>*Helmut Walcha (1907-1991)*

Bach is a musician-painter and not a musician-poet.
>*Albert Schweitzer (1875-1965)*

Mozart is the greatest composer known to me personally or by name.
>*Joseph Haydn (1732-1809)*

Mozart is the human incarnation of the divine force of creation.
>*Johann W. von Goethe (1749-1832)*

I produce music as an apple-tree produces apples.
>*Camille Saint-Saëns (1835-1921)*

There is no law against composing music when one has no ideas whatsoever. The music of Wagner, therefore, is perfectly legal.
    The National, *Paris, 1850*

Thomas Mann, listenng to the Twilight of the Gods on his radio in Zurich, suddenly left the room in disgust: "Nothing that comes from there is innocent; there's cultural propaganda behind it all".
    Brigitte Hamann (1940-   )

The cymbal is one of the oldest musical instruments. Ordinary cymbals don't have any particular tonality. All cymbals, like brandy, improve with age. There are fourteen kinds of cymbals: splash, crash, fast-crash, swish, bounce, bebop, concert-band, brass-band, symphony, fast, hi-hat, flange-hi-hat, ride and finger.
    The New Yorker, *13.8.1949*

The recorder derives its name from an archaic meaning of the verb 'record', that is, 'to sing like a bird'.
    Time, *15.7.1966*

I occasionally play works by contemporary composers and for two reasons. First, to discourage the composer from writing any more and secondly to remind myself how much I appreciate Beethoven.
    Jascha Heifetz (1901-1987)

Every composer knows the anguish and despair occasioned by forgetting ideas which one has no time to write down.
    Hector Berlioz (1803-1869)
    [The same can be said of writers. LZ]

Beethoven regularly broke strings when playing his own works.
    Richard Burnett

The metronome was invented in 1812 by Dietrich Nikolaus Winkel of Amsterdam. However, he did not receive proper credit, because Johann Neponuk Maelzel of Vienna patented the device in 1816 and claimed to be the inventor. Until today, the indication M.M. plus a number in music scores indicates the tempo as in Maelzel's Metronome.

An opera is where somebody gets stabbed in the back and instead of bleeding, he sings.

It is easier to understand a nation by listening to its music than by learning its language.

The visiting quartet played Brahms. Brahms lost.

MYTHS

Whatever Oedipus may have done - and however we interpret it - the simple fact is that Oedipus's parents began the whole business by trying to kill Oedipus.
Anthony Wilden (1935-   )

MYSTICISM

The ineffable really exists, it is shown, not said; it's the mystic.
Ludwig Wittgenstein (188-1951)

We have a tendency not to reason, but to mystery; not to the penetrating and clear thought, but to sorcery; not to the human intellect searching for explanation but to the gnostic omniscience in the absurd; not to science but to sorcery behind scientific masks; not to activity founded on reasoning, but on magic.
Karl Jaspers (1883-1969)

There is no need for temples, no need for complicated philosophy. Our own brain, our own heart is our temple; the philosophy is kindness.
Dalai Lama (1935-   )

NASTY PEOPLE

A bad temper never mellows with age, and a sharp tongue is the only edged tool that grows keener with constant use.
Washington Irving (1783-1859)

Stalin and Henry Ford could have understood one anther perfectly.
Aldous Huxley (1894-1963)

A sense of duty is useful in work, but offensive in personal relations.
Bertrand Russell (1872-1970)

Money doesn't buy class.
Or, in Spanish: Lo que Natura non da Salamanca non presta
(What Nature didn't bestow, Education won't lend) LZ.

He's the kind of person who makes you wish birth control was retroactive.

NATURE

Nature is a structure of evolutionary processes. The reality is the process.
Alfred North Whitehead (1861-1947)

Nature does not bestow virtue; to be good is an art.
Seneca (4 BCE-65 CE)

Art makes visible the nature of things.
Rudolph Arnheim (1904-2007)

Nature itself invites us to be Geometricians.
Christian Huygens (1629-1695)

Nature uses as little as possible of anything.
Johannes Kepler (1571-1630)

No bird soars too high, if he soars with his own wings.
William Blake (1757-1827)

The tree which moves some to tears of joy is in the eyes of others only a green thing that stands in the way. Some see nature all ridicule and deformity... and some scarce see nature at all. But to the eyes of the man of imagination, nature is imagination itself.
William Blake (1757-1827)

In nature there are neither rewards nor punishments; there are consequences.
Robert Green Ingersoll (1833-1879)

He loves nature in spite of what it did to him.
Forrest Tucker (1919-1986)

In the physical world, one cannot increase the size or quantity of anything without changing its quality. Similar figures exist only in pure geometry.
Paul Valéry (1871-1945)

Repetition is the only form of permanence that nature can achieve.
George Santayana (1863-1952)

What is a miracle? The natural law of a unique event.
  Eugen Rosenstock-Huessy (1888-1973)

Nature loves hiding itself. (*Physis Krypthesistoi Philei*)

Mother nature is a bitch.

NEWSPAPERS

Trying to determine what is going on in the world by reading a newspaper is like trying to tell the time by reading the second-hand of a clock.
  Ben Hecht (1894-1964)

The man who reads nothing at all is better educated than the man who reads nothing but newspapers
  Thomas Jefferson (1743-1826)

With the press there is no "off the record"
  Donald Rumsfeld (1932-   )

Trying to be a first-rate reporter on the average American newspaper is like trying to play Bach's 'St. Maththew's Passion' on a ukelele.
  Ben Bagdikian (1920-   )

New news every day ... of what these tempestuous times afford ... of wars, plagues, fires, inundations, massacres, meteors ... so many men slain ... new pamphlets, currantoes ... controversies.
  Robert Burton (1577-1640), commenting the shattering effect on contemporary nerves of the news of the day (1624, the year of the belated English entry into the Thirty years War)

Newspaper editors are men who separate the wheat from the chaff, and then print the chaff.
  Adlai Stevenson (1900-1965)

American media...would seem to be expressly devised by the great agent of mischief, to depress and destroy all that is good and to elevate and advance all that is evil in the nation.
  James Fenimore Cooper (1789-1851)

Newspapers are to books as a circus band is to a symphony orchestra.
  Leon Zeldis

NEW YEAR

In the Hebrew language, *Tishri* marks the New Year for counting years, while *Nisan* for counting months. *Shana* [year] comes from the same root as *Sheni* or *Mishna*, to repeat, while *Hodesh* [month] is from the same root as *Hadash*, new (i.e. the new moon).

The same letters of '*Alef betishri*' (First day of *Tishri*, start of the Hebrew year) can be arranged to form the word '*Bereshit*', the first word of the Bible.

NEW YORK

A considerable part of New York is nothing more than a provisional city, a city which will be replaced by another city.
> *Le Corbusier (1887-1965)*

New York: where everybody mutinies but no one deserts.
> *Harry Hershfield (1885-1974)*

I think that's how Chicago got started. A bunch of people in New York said, 'Gee, I'm enjoying the crime and the poverty, but it just isn't cold enough. Let's go west.'
> *Richard Jeni (1957-2007)*

If you live in New York, even if you're Catholic, you're Jewish.
> *Lenny Bruce (1923-1966)*

I think my favorite sport in the Olympics is the one in which you make your way through the snow, you stop, you shoot a gun, and then you continue. In most of the world, it is known as biathlon, except in New York City, where it is known as winter.
> *Michael Ventre*

NONSENSE

Nonsense may indeed be nonsense, but the study of nonsense is not.
> *Gershom Scholem (1897-1982)*

For blocks are better cleft with wedges,
Than tools of sharp or softer edges,
And dullest nonsense had been found
By some to be to most profound.
> *Samuel Butler (1612-1680)*

A little nosense now and then
Is relished by the best of men.

NOSTALGIA

I feel nostalgia for a time when the world was thought to be more benign, when tea was tea and not a dangerous stimulant, when God had our best interests at heart and we could relax and forget about our fate. Nowadays, anyone alive is slightly ill by definition.
>   *Hugo Williams (1942-   )*

Nostalgia isn't what it used to be.
>   *Peter de Vries (1910-1993)*

Photographs actively promote nostalgia.
>   *Susan Sontag (1933-2004)*

NUCLEAR WAR

If you have seen one nuclear war, you have seen them all.
>   *Bob Muron*

OBSCENITY

I know it when I see it.
>   *Justice Potter Stewart (1915-1985)*

OBTUSENESS

Minds are like parachutes, They only function when they are open.
>   *Sir James Dewar (1842-1923)*

The wheel's spinning but the hamster's dead.

Proof that evolution CAN go in reverse.

He who laughs last, thinks slowest.

Light travels faster than sound. This is why some people appear bright until you hear them speak.

He is so dense he absorbs neutrinos.

Everyone has a photographic memory. Some don't have film.

OEDIPUS

Whatever Oedipus may have done - and however we interpret it - the simple fact is that Oedipus's parents began the whole business by trying to kill Oedipus.
Anthony Wilden (1935-   )

Oedipus, schmoedipus, what does it matter so long as the boy loves his mother?
Jewish joke

OLD AGE

Old age is not so bad when you consider the alternative.
Maurice Chevalier (1888-1972), at age 72

Old myths, old gods, old heroes have never died. They are only sleeping at the bottom of our mind, waiting for our call. We have need for them. They represent the wisdom of our race.
Stanley Kunitz (1905-   ), at age 79

The years teach many things the days never know.
Ralpth Waldo Emerson (1803-1882)

All lovely things will have an ending,
All lovely things will fade and die,
And youth, that's now so bravely spending,
Will beg a penny by and by.
Conrad Aiken (1889-1973)

The older I grow the more I distrust the familiar doctrine that age brings wisdom.
H. L. Mencken (1880-1956)

A man who is always living in the midst of his studies and labors does not perceive when old age creeps upon him.
Cato the Elder (234-149 BCE), at age 83

Oneiropause, worse than menopause: end of mental ovulation.
Jean Baudrillard (1929-   )

Statesmen and beauties are very rarely sensible to the gradations of their decay.

> *Earl of Chesterfield (1694-1773)*

Youth is a blunder; manhood a struggle; old age a regret.

> *Benjamin Disraeli (1804-1881)*

Inside every older person is a younger persons wondering what the heck happened.

> *Cora Harvey Armstrong*

It is not only a question of works never to be written. It is a matter of things unlearned. I have started to learn Japanese, but it is too late; I have started to read Hebrew, but my eyes will not take in the jots and tittles. How can one fade out in peace, carrying vast ignorance into a state of total ignorance?

> *Anthony Burgess (1917-1993)*

In the eyes of the young burns the flame, but in the eyes of the old glows the light.

> *Victor Hugo (1802-1885)*

The young man knows the rules but the old man knows the exceptions.

> *Oliver Wendell Holmes (1809-1894)*

It is true that the old have no opportunities, no possibilities in the future. But they have more than that. Instead of possibilities in the future, they have realities in the past – the potentialities they have realized – and nothing and nobody can ever remove those assets from the past.

> *Viktor E. Frankl (1905-1997).*
> *[cf. "Lo comido y lo bailado no me lo quita nadie" – What I ate and what I danced, nobody can take away. Argentinean saying. LZ]*

I must reluctantly observe that two causes, the abbreviation of time and the failure of hope, will always tinge with a browner shade the evening of life.

> *Edward Gibbon (1737-1794)*

Of late I appear
To have reached that stage
When people look old
Who are only my age.

> *Richard Armour (1906-1989)*

156

You are an old timer if youy can remember when setting the world on fire was a figure of speech.
> *Franklin P. Jones*

Henri, Duc d'Aumale, French aristocrat son of King Louis Philippe, was renowned for his youthful love affairs, but as an old man, he felt his powers failing. 'As a yong man, I used to have four supple members and one stiff one,' he sadly observed. 'Now, I have four stiff and one supple.'

With age the soul, like paper, becomes parched, wrinkled and creaky.
> *Leon Zeldis*

There are three problems with old age: bad memory is one, and there are two others.
> *Leon Zeldis*

OPENING REMARKS

The secret of a good speaker is to remember three things: speak loudly, so they can hear you; speak slowly, so they understand you, and speak shortly, so they invite you again.
> *General José Berdichewsky*

I take the view, and always have, that if you cannot say what you are going to say in twenty minutes, you ought to go away and write a book about it.
> *Lord Brabazon (1884-1964)*

Here comes the Orador! With his flood of words, and his drop of reason.
> *Benjamin Franklin (1706-1790)*

I feel like one of the seven husbands of Elizabeth Taylor. I know what I have to do, but the difficulty is keeping it interesting.

The secret of a good speech is to have a good beginning, a good ending, and keeping both close together.

Public speaking is like drilling for oil: if you haven't hit something in twenty minutes, it's time to quit boring.

OPINION

Men never think their fortunes too great, nor their wit too little.
> *Thomas Fuller (1608-1661)*

Every new opinion, at its starting, is precisely in a minority of one.
    Thomas Carlyle (1795-1881)

In matters of opinion, our adversaries are insane.
    Oscar Wilde (1854-1900)

The man who never alters his opinion is like standing water and breeds reptiles of the mind.
    William Blake (1757-1827)

It isn't what people think that is important, but the rason they think what they think.
    Eugene Ionescu (1912-1994)

Keep an open mind, you never know when something might fall in.
    Benny Sewell

One must judge men, not by their opinions, but by what their opinions have made of them.
    Georg Christoph Lichtenberg (1742-1799)

Man is a gregarious animal, and much more so in his mind than in his body. He may like to go alone for a walk, but he hates to stand alone in his opinions.
    George Santayana (1863-1952)

Opinions are proposed, not imposed.
    Pope John Paul II (1920-2005)

Those who never retract their opinions love themselves more than they love the truth.
    Joseph Joubert (1754-1824)

The more intelligent a man is, the more originality he discovers in men. Ordinary people see no difference between men.
    Blaisé Pascal (1623-1662)

Some people are not persuasive, but contagious.
    Paul Claudel (1868-1955)

No one can have a higher opinion of him than I have, and I think he's a dirty little beast.
    W.S. Gilbert (1836-1911)

When I want your opinion, I'll give it to you.
Dr. Laurence J. Peter (1919-1990)

Every man takes the limits of his own field of vision for the limits of the world.
Arthur Schoppenhauer (1788-1860)

In all the facets in a diamond were cut parallel, the stone would have no life.

Without opinion there could be no art.
Leon Zeldis

OPPORTUNITY

When one door closes another door opens; but we so often look so long and so regrestfully upon the closed door, that we do not see the ones which open for us.
Alexander Graham Bell (1847-1922)

The lure of the distant and the different is deceptive.
The great opportunity is where you are.
John Burroughs (1837-1921)

Opportunity knocks only once, but what if it knocks you down?
Leon Zeldis

OPTIMISM

The pessimist complains about the wind;
The optimist expects it to change;
The realist trims the sails.
William Arthur Ward (1921-1997)

The American people never carry an umbrella. They prepare to walk in eternal sunshine.
Alfred E. Smith (1873-1944)

Being defeated is often a temporary condition. Giving up makes it permanent.
Marlene vos Savant

Although I know we have already grown accustomed to less beauty, less elegance, less excellence, yet perversely I have confidence in the opposite of egalitarianism; in the competence and excellence of the best among us. The urge for the best is an element of humankind as inherent as the heartbeat. It may be crushed temporarily but it cannot be eliminated. If incompetence does not kill us first, we will win. We will always have pride in accomplishment, the charm of fine things - and we will win horse races. As long as people exist, some will always strive for the best. And some will attain it.

Barbara Tuchman (1912-1989)

Finish each day and be done with it. You have done what you could. Some blunders and absurdities no doubt crept in; forget them as soon as you can. Tomorrow is a new day; begin it well and serenely and with too high a spirit to be encumbered with your old nonsense.

Ralph Waldo Emerson (1803-1882)

Life is to be lived, not controlled, and humanity is won by continuing to play in the face of certain defeat.

Ralph Ellison (1914-1994)

The optimist proclaims that we live in the best of all worlds; and the pessimist fears this is true.

Branch Cabell (1879-1958)

Too many people overvalue what they are not and undervalue what they are.

Malcolm Forbes (1919-1990)

A man who is a pessimist before forty-eight knows too much, if he is an optimist after it, he knows too little.

Mark Twain (1835-1910)

I am an optimist. It does not seem of much use being anything else.

Winston Churchill (1874-1965)

There is no fate that cannot be surmounted by scorn.

Albert Camus (1913-1960)

If at first you don't succeed, failure may be your style.

Quentin Crisp (1908-1999)

If you can smile when everything is going wrong, it's because you already found whom to blame.

OXFORD

Whatever people may say against Cambridge, it is certainly the best preparatory school for Oxford that I know.
Oscar Wilde (1854-1900)

OXYMORONS

Include me out.
Samuel Goldwyn (1882-1974)

We are going to turn this team around 360 degrees.
Jason Kidd (1973-   )

Act naturally. Same difference. Almost exactly. Sanitary landfill. Living dead. Business ethics. Military Inteligence. New classic. Peace force. Pretty ugly. Diet ice cream. Exact estimate. Microsoft Works.

An honest politician.
Leon Zeldis

PAIN

Even when you have pain, you don't have to be one.
Maya Angelou (1928-   )

PAINTING

To see a painting is to hear it: understand what it says. Painting is also music, and above all language.
Octavio Paz (1914-1998)

When one is painting one does not think.
Raphael (1483-1520)

Offensive objects, at a proper distance, acquire even a degree of beauty.
William Shenstone (1714-1763)

Painting is a science, and should be pursued as an inquiry into the laws of nature. Why, then, may not landscape painting be considered a branch of natural philosophy, of which pictures are but the experiments?
John Constable (1776-1837)

It is better to paint from memory, for thus your work will be your own; your sensation, your intelligence, and your soul will triumph over the eye of the amateur... Do not finish your work too much.
Paul Gaugin (1848-1903)

There is no such a thing as good painting about nothing.
Mark Rothko (1903-1970)

One always has to spoil a picture a little bit in order to finish it.
Eugéne Delacroix (1798-1863)

One line has no meaning; a second one is needed to give it expression.
Eugéne Delacroix (1798-1863)

A painting is never finished – it simply stops in interesting places.
Paul Gardner (1954-   )

An art of symbols always evolves into a language of decoration.
Sir Kenneth Clark (1903-1983)

He who pretends to be either painter or engraver without being a master of drawing is an impostor.
William Blake (1757-1827)

Taste is the death of a painter.
Walter Sickert (1860-1942)

That which, perhaps, hears more silly remarks than anything else in the world, is a picture in a museum.
The Goncourt brothers (1822-1896 and 1830-1870)

Expressionist painter: one who shouts with the eyes.
Leon Zeldis

PALINDROMES

Sex at noon taxes.
Sator opera arepo rotas.
A man, a plan, a canal: Panama.

PARADOX

There is nothing so unpredictable as the past.
Declan Donnellan (1953)

162

PARIS

I think that Paris is a beautiful city with the ugliest things, while London is an ugly city with very beautiful things.
Montesquieu (1689-1755)

In 1836, there were 18,000 prostitutes in Paris; by the end of the century 20 percent of the population of the city were afftected by syphilis.
Virginia Rounding

PARKINSON'S LAW

Work expands so as to fill the time available for its completion.
C. Northcote Parkinson (1909-1993)

PEARLS

Cultivated pearls were developed by Kokichi Mikimoto starting in 1889. The first ones were not round, but semicircular in shape. Black pearls are made by radiating ordinary pearls with gamma rays from Cobalt 60 during some 16 hours.

PERFECTION

This is the very perfection of a man, to find out his own imperfections.
St. Augustine (354-430)

Better a diamond with a flaw than a pebble without.
Confucius (c. 551-479)

The greater the emphasis on perfection, the further it recedes.
Haridas Chaudhuri (1913-1975)

Perfection does not exist. To understand this is the triumph of human intelligence; to expect to possess it is the most dangerous kind of madness.
Alfred de Musset (1810-1857)

Waiting until everything is perfect before making a move is like waiting to start a trip until all the traffic lights are green.
Karen Ireland (1977-   )

PERSONALITY

One merely wanders round and round within the circle of one's personality.
>   *Oscar Wilde (1854-1900)*

Every man lives behind bars, which he carries within him.
>   *Franza Kafka (1883-1924)*

You may be only one person for the world, but for some person you are all the world.
>   *Gabriel García Márquez (1928-   )*

Many are stubborn in the pursuit of the path they have chosen, few in pursuit of the goal.
>   *Nietzsche (1844-1900)*

Men are anxious to improve their circumstances, but are unwilling to improve themselves, they therefore remain bound.
>   *James Allen (1864-1912)*

Each has his past shut in him like the leaves of a book known to him by heart, and his friends can only read the title.
>   *Virginia Woolf (1882-1941)*

Always remember you are unique, just like everyone else.

PERSPECTIVE

The hen is an egg's way of producing another egg.
>   *Samuel Butler (1835-1902)*

It is the sick oyster which possesses the pearl.
>   *J. A. Shedd*

My Mom said she learned how to swim when someone took her out in the lake and then threw her off the boat. I said, 'Mom, they weren't trying to teach you how to swim'.
>   *Paula Poundstone (1959-   )*

The lion, the panther and the tiger are harmless animals. The bird, the chicken and the dove are dangerous animals.
That's the advice of a mother worm to her child.

PESSIMISM

A pessimist is someone who complains about the noise when opportunity knocks.
> *Michael Levine*

The optimist proclaims that we live in the best of all worlds; and the pessimist fears this is true.
> *Branch Cabell (1879-1958)*

Sometimes I get the feeling that the whole world is against me, but deep down I know that's not true. Some smaller countries are neutral.
> *Robert Orben*

The pessimist complains about the wind;
The optimist expects it to change;
The realist adjusts the sails.
> *William Arthur Ward (1921-1997)*

It is never so bad it can't get worse.
> *Yiddish saying*

A man who suffers before it is necessary, suffers more than necessary.
> *Seneca (4 BCE-65 CE)*

At the bottom of the modern man there is always a great thirst for self-forgetfulness, self-distraction... and therefore he turns away from all those problems and abysses which might recall to him his own nothingness.
> *Henri Frédéric Amiel (1821-1881)*

The best of men cannot suspend their fate:
The good die early, and the bad die late.
> *Daniel Defoe (1660-1731)*

They are ill discoverers that think there is no land, when they can see nothing but sea.
> *Francis Bacon (1561-1626)*

A pessimist is one who looks at both sides before crossing a one-way street.

A pessimist sees every problem through a macroscope.
> *Leon Zeldis*

PHILISTINE

Philistine appears in English in the 17th century. Matthew Arnold in his essay on Heinrich Heine, among his *"Essays in Criticism"* (1865), first used the word in the way it is now accepted, the enemy of culture who is, in Arnold's words, "inaccessible and impatient to ideas".

Apparently he derived this meaning from the Biblical passage: "All the wells which his father's servants had dug in the days of Abraham his father, the Philistines had stopped and filled with earth" (Gen. 26, 15).

Louis I. Rabinowitz

PHILOSOPHY

The scientific ideal has become the target of all knowledge and the only legitimate means of accessing reality.

Martin Heidegger (1889-1976)

Making itself intelligible is suicide for philosophy.

Martin Heidegger (1889-1976)

All metaphysical books should be burned as nothing but sophistry and illusion.

David Hume (1711-1776)

Bertrand Russell once referred to Kant as the greatest catastrophe in the history of philosophy. C. D. Broad commented that this position surely belonged to Hegel. Russell and Broad were wrong, because the title undountedly belongs to Martin Heidegger.

Paul Edwards (1923-2004)

Children never play to distract themselves, but to concentrate. The same is true of philosophers.

Fernando Savater (1947-   )

There is no need for temples, no need for complicated philosophy. Our own brain, our own heart is our temple; the philosophy is kindness.

Dalai Lama (1935-   )

A philosophical fashion catches on like a gastronomical fashion; one can no more refute an idea than a sauce.

E. Michel Cioran (1911-1995)

Science is what you know, philosophy is what you don't know.

Bertrand Russell (1872-1970)

All of us tend to put off living. We are all dreaming of some magical rose garden over the horizon instead of enjoying the roses that are blooming outside our window today.
> *Dale Carnegie (1888-1955)*

Events do not harm you, but their perception may do.
> *Epictetus (1ˢᵗ-2ⁿᵈ c.)*

There is only one really serious philosophical problem, namely suicide.
> *Albert Camus (1913-1960)*

Things are not as they seem, nor are they otherwise.
> *Buddhist Sutra*

Ontology is what kinds of facts there are; semantics, what kinds of truths there are; epistemology, what ways there are of knowing truths.
> *Jerry Foder*

I hear and I forget. I see and I remember. I do and I understand.
> *Confucius (551-479 BCE)*

One must first discipline and control one's own mind. If a man can control his own mind he will find the way to enlightenment and all wisdom and virtue will naturally come to him.
> *Gautama Buddha (563?-453? BCE)*

We don't see things as they are, we see things as we are.
> *Steve Feite*

Events do not harm you, but their perception may do.
> *Epictetus (1ˢᵗ-2ⁿᵈ CE)*

Nature is a structure of evolutionary processes. The reality is the process.
> *Alfred North Whitehead (1861-1947)*

Mocking philosophy is really doing philosophy.
> *Pascal (1623-1662)*

Philosophy alone makes the mind invincible, and places us out of reach of fortune, so that all her arrows fall short of us.
> *Seneca (4 BCE-65 CE)*

Mr. Wittgenstein manages to say a good deal about what cannot be said.
> *Bertrand Russell (1872-1970)*

167

It is a sad fact about my profession, wonderful though it is, that the most famous and admired philosophers are often the ones with the most preposterous theories.
John Searle (1932-   )

Cassius Dio accused Seneca of a hypocritical failure to live his life in accordance with his philosophy. "While denouncing tyranny, he made himself the teacher of a tyrant...Though criticizing the rich, he acquired a fortune of three million sesterces". He also had affairs with married women and young boys.
Emily Wilson

One ought, every day at least, to hear a little song, read a good poem, see a fine picture and, if it were possible, speak a few reasonable words.
Johann Wolfgang von Goethe(1749-1832)

To do philosophy, it is not to be a spectator of philosophy, but to act philosophy.
Henry Corbin (1903-1978)

Once the concept of infinity has been taken seriously, a human dwelling can no longer be made of the universe. The universe can still be thought but it can no longer be imagined, the man who thinks it no longer really lives in it.
Martin Buber (1878-1965)

The primary task of philosophy of religion is to rediscover the questions to which religion is an answer. In our quest for forgotten questions, the method and spirit of philosophical inquiry are of greater importance than theology. Theology starts with dogma, philosophy begins with problems. Philosophy saees the problem first, theology has the answer in advance.
Rabbi Abraham Joshua Heschel (1907-1972)

Nietzsche was stupid and abnormal.
Leo Tolstoy (1818-1910)

To philosophize is to learn to die.
Jacques Derrida (1930-2004)

The job of philosophy, since Plato, is concerned with truth, goodness and beauty. That is logic and epistemology, ethics and esthetics.

Three years after the General Theory of Relativity was verified by Eddington, ending belief in fixed space and time, Ludwig Wittgenstein published his *Tractatus Logico-Philosophicus*, which cumulatively over the decades destroyed confidence in systematic philosophy as a guide to human reason.

PHYSICIANS see also MEDICINE

He cures most in whom most have faith.
> *Galen (130?-201?)*

Wherever a doctor cannot do good, he must be kept from doing harm.
> *Hippocrates (460?-377? BCE)*

Don't ask the doctor; ask the patient.
> *Yiddish proverb*

Care more for the individual patient than for the special features of the disease.
> *Sir William Osler (1849-1919)*

The relation between psychiatrists and other kinds of lunatic is more or less the relation of a convex folly to a concave one.
> *Karl Kraus (1874-1936)*

Doctors allow us to die; charlatans kill us.
> *La Bruyere, Jean de (1645-1696)*

POETS & POETRY

There cannot be, there ought not to be, *lyric* poetry after Auschwitz.
> *Theodor W. Adorno (1903-1969)*

I have seen all the pictures from Buchenwald – it's impossible to be a poet any longer.
> *Halldór Laxness (1902-1998)*

Most wretched men
Are cradled into poetry by wrong,
They learn in suffering what they teach in song.
> *George Gordon, Lord Byron (1788-1824)*

Without surrealism there can be no poetry.
> *Nicanor Parra (1915-   )*

Sir, I admit your general rule
that every poet is a fool;
but you yourself may serve to show it,
that every fool is not a poet.
> *Alexander Pope (1688-1744)*

This poem will never reach its destination.
> *Voltaire (1694-1778) on Rousseau's* Ode to Posterity

What the heart could love as poetry,
reason can love as philosophy.
> *Wallace Stevens, writing about Delmore Schwartz*

Poetry is putting the infinite within the finite.
> *Robert Browning (1812-1889)*

Poetry is as exact a science as geometry.
> *Gustave Flaubert (1821-1880)*

Poetry is to prose as dancing is to walking.
> *John Barrington Wain (1925-1994)*

Any good poem is inexhaustible, like a human being.
> *Novalis (1772-1801)*

I'll stay off Verlain too: he was always chasing Rimbauds.
> *Dorothy Parker (1893-1967)*

The genuine poet is always a priest.
> *Novalis (1772-1801)*

Any fool can get into a poem but it takes a poet to get out of one.
> *Attributed to Robert Frost (1874-1963)*

Not marble nor the gilded monuments
of princes shall outlive this powerful rhyme.
> *William Shakespeare (1564-1616)*

Shakespeare was occupied with turning human actions into poetry.
> *T.S. Eliot (1888-1965)*

And as imagination bodies forth
The form of things unknown, the poet's pen
Turns them, shapes, and gives to airy nothing
A local habitation and a name.
  William Shakespeare (1564-1616).

Immature poets imitate, mature poets steal.
  T. S. Eliot (1888-1965)

Poets and historians are the best doctors.
  Francis Bacon (1561-1626)

The lunatic, the lover and the poet
Are of imagination all compact.
  William Shakespeare (1564-1616)

Poetry is the revelation of a feeling that the poet believes to be interior
and personal, but which the reader recognizes as his own.
  Salvatore Quasimodo (1901-1968)

Poetry has its roots in human breathing - and what would we be if our
breath diminished?
  George Seferis (1900-1971)

I know from experience that even if some poets are often quoted, they are
seldom read.
  George Seferis (1900-1971)

Seferis has the ability to let drop observations about life and poetry which
tumble into the mind like pebbles down an empty well and echo on for
years.
  Lawrence Durrell (1912-1990)

The poem is a lengthy vacillation between sound and meaning.
  Paul Valéry (1871-1945)

A poem is never finished, only abandoned.
  Paul Valéry (1871-1945)

We must be clear that, when it comes to atoms, language can be used only
as in poetry.
  Niels Bohr (1885-1962)

Either engineers must become poets, or the poets must become engineers.
Norbert Wiener (1894-1964))

Poets have an enthusiasm similar to that of prophets and fortune-tellers, who all say very good things, without understanding a word of what they say.
Socrates (470?-399 BCE)

Some poems lose something in the original.
John McInnes

Herder's *Kalligone* is rant, abuse, drunken self-conceit that kicking and sprawling in the 6 inch-deep Gutter of muddy Philosophism from the drainings of a hundred sculleries dreams that he is swimming in an ocean of the Translucent & the Profound.
Samuel Taylor Coleridge (1772-1834)

The successful Symbolist poem is one in which sound, and color, and form are in a musical relation, a beautiful relation to one another, ... where they become, as it were, one sound, one color, one form, and evoke an emotion that is made out of their distinct evocations and yet is one emotion.
William Butler Yeats (1865-1939)

My idea is renewing Music through its most intimate alliance with Poetry.
Franz Liszt (1811-1886)

The world must be romanticized.
Novalis - Friedrich von Hardenberg (1772-1801)

Dream and fantasy are our most unique possessions.
Novalis (1772-1801)

The poet is the medium of nature.
Federico García Lorca (1899-1936)

Publishing a volume of verse is like dropping a rose petal down the Grand Canyon and waiting for the echo.
Don Marquis (1878-1937)

The four subjects of poetry:
  1.   I went into the woods today, and it made me feel, you know, sort of religious.

2. We are not getting any younger.
3. It sure is cold and lonely (a) without you, honey, or (b) with you, honey.
4. Sadness seems but the other side of the coin of happiness, and vice-versa, and in any case, the coin is too soon spent, and on what we know not.
William Matthews (1942-1997)

Writing a poem is like opening a present. We assume there is something nice inside, perhaps beautiful, but until we finish unwrapping it, we'll never know.
Leon Zeldis

Every poet is a mystic *manqué*.
Leon Zeldis

Poetry is an asymptotic road to truth.
Leon Zeldis

The art of the poet is to make a forest out of a few trees.
Leon Zeldis

POLITICALLY CORRECT

Being called a poetess brings out the terroristress in me.
Audre Lorde

He's not dead, he's encephalographically challenged.

He's an experiment in artificial stupidity.

Experientially enhanced (old people).

Once he stopped to think, and forgot to start again.

He achieved a deficiency (he failed).

Pitiful result of the anti-abortion laws.

Why men can only be cute, while women can be beautiful?
Leon Zeldis

POLITICS

I will not deny that there are men in the district better qualified than I to go to Congress, but gentlemen, these men are not in the race.
Sam Rayburn (1882-1961)

One of the penalties for refusing to participate in politics is that you end up being governed by your inferiors.
Plato (427?-347 BCE)

The word politics is derived from the word "poly", meaning many, and the word "ticks" meaning blood-sucking parasites.
Larry Hardiman

A nation that draws too broad a difference between its scholars and its warriors will have its thinking being done by cowards and its fighting by fools.
Thucydides (460-400 BCE)

Politics is not the art of the possible. It consists in choosing between the disastrous and the unpalatable.
John Kenneth Galbraith (1908-   )

When they call the roll in the Senate, the Senators do not know whether to answer "Present" or "Nor Guilty".
Theodore Roosevelt (1958-1919)

Against bodies, violence; against souls, lies.
The ruling principle of Serge Netchayev (1847-1882), Russian revolutionary disciple of Bakunin, mentor of Lenin

Comunism, like any other revealed religion, is largely made up of prophesies.
H. L. Mencken (1880-1956)

A nationalist is one who has a small love and a great hatred.
André Gide (1869-1951)

A communist is someone who has read Marx; an anti-communist is someone who understood Marx.
Ronald Reagan (1911-2004)

Politics is supposed to be the second oldest profession in the world. I reached the conclusion that it is greatly similar to the first.
> *Ronald Reagan (1911-2004)*

It is not by the goodness of butchers, bakers and vintners that we have our dinner, but by their self interest.
> *Adam Smith (1723-1790)*

The people who cast the votes don't decide an election; the people who count the votes do.
> *Joseph Stalin (1879-1952)*

Silence, please, citizens; for I know better than you what is good for the Republic.
> *P. Scipio Nasica, Roman Consul in 191 BCE*
> *[No change from Roman times to our own. LZ]*

I never vote for anyone. I always vote against.
> *W. C. Fields (1880-1946)*

A politician is a man who will double cross that bridge when he comes to it.
> *Oscar Levant (1906-1972)*

What this country needs is more unemployed politicians.
> *Edward Langley (1928-1995)*

The problem with political jokes is that they get elected.
> *Henry Cate VII*

Ninety percent of the politicians give the other ten percent a bad reputation.
> *Henry Kissinger (1923-   )*

All significant concepts of the modern theory of the state are secularized theological concepts.
> *Carl Schmitt (1888-1985)*

A liberal is someone who feels a great debt to society, which he proposes to pay off with your money.
> *G. Gordon Liddy (1930-   )*

Idealism is fine, but as it approaches reality, the cost becomes prohibitive.
> *William F. Buckley Jr. (1925-2008)*

I am a Conservative to preserve all that is good in our constitution, a Radical to remove all that is bad. I seek to preserve property and to respect order, and I equally decry the appeal to the passions of the many or the prejudices of the few.

> *Benjamin Disraeli (1804-1881)*

When buying and selling are controlled by legislation, the first thing to be bought and sold are legislators.

> *P. J. O'Rourke (1947-   )*

A billion here, a billion there, pretty soon it adds up to real money.

> *US Senator Everett Dirksen (1896-1969)*

No man's life, liberty or prosperity is safe while the legislature is in session.

> *Mark Twain (1835-1910)*

Suppose you were an idiot, and suppose you were a member of Congress. But, I repeat myself.

> *Mark Twain (1835-1910)*

Politics is the art of looking for problems, finding them, making an erroneous diagnostic and then applying the wrong remedies.

> *Groucho Marx (1895-1977)*

In our civilization, and under our republican form of government, intelligence is so highly honored that its is rewarded by exemption from the cares of office.

> *Ambrose Bierce (1842-1914)*

It is not enough to have every intelligent person in the country voting for me. I need a majority.

> *Adlai Stevenson (1900-1965)*
> *[He lost the presidential election. LZ]*

I have been told I was on the road to hell, but I had no idea it was just a mile down the road with a Dome on it.

> *Abraham Lincoln (1809-1865)*

Few are ready to recognize that the birth of Fascism and Nazism was not a reaction against the socialist tendencies of the preceding period, but the inevitable product of those movements.

> *Friedrich Hayek (1899-1992)*

The difference between a politician and a statesman is: a politician thinks of the next election and a statesman thinks of the next generation.
James Freeman Clarke (1810-1888)

The Democratic Party is like a mule - without pride of ancestry or hope of posterity.
Edmund Burke (1729-1797)

An ancient Egyptian copy of a 1269 BCE peace treaty signed between Hittite King Hattushili and Pharaoh Ramses II, fifteen years after a battle in what is now Syria, gives an insight into the unchanging nature of politicians.

It refers to the Hittite ruler as inferior to Ramses II. But the original documents exchanged between the rulers, which have also been found, carried phrases giving each equal standing.

'Politics was no different even then,' Alp (Turkish archeologist Sedat Alp) said. 'We believe the mutually agreed text was changed by Ramses to boost himself politically in his own country'.
Jerusalem Post, *11.4.1990*

An honest politician is one who, when he is bought, will stay bought.
Simon Cameron (1799-1889)

Nothing doth more hurt in a state than that cunning men pass for wise.
Francis Bacon (1561-1626)

Politics, and the fate of mankind, are shaped by men without ideals and without greatness.
Albert Camus (1913-1960)

In politics, as in high finance, duplicity is regarded as a virtue.
Mikhail A. Bakunin (1814-1876)

Despotism tempered by assassination - that is our Magna Charta.
Anonymous Russian

How often it happens, that, when a catastrophe occurs, if we inquire into the cause, we find it originated through the obstinacy of one with little ability, but having full faith in his own powers.
Victor Hugo (1802-1885)

Being powerful is like being a lady. If you have to tell people you are, you aren't.
Margaret Thatcher (1925-)

Men in power are so anxious to establish the myth of infallibility that they do their utmost to ignore truth.
> *Boris Pasternak (1890-1960)*

All parties, without exception, what they seek for power are varieties of absolutism.
> *Pierre Prudhon (1809-1865)*

What men most value in this world is not rights but privileges.
> *H. L. Mencken (1880-1956)*

[A candidate] is asked to stand, he wants to sit, he is expected to lie.
> *Winston Churchill (1874-1965)*

He is a modest man who has a good deal to be modest about.
> *Winston Churchill (1874-1965), about Clement Atlee.*

The inherent vice of capitalism is the unequal sharing of blessings; the inherent virtue of socialism is the equal sharing of miseries.
> *Winston Churchill (1874-1965)*
> *[For once Churchill was wrong. Most people in "socialist" (i.e. communist) countries are indeed miserable, but the select party members live in luxury. LZ]*

No socialist system can be established without a political police.
> *Winston Churchill (1874-1965)*

He occasionally stumbled over the truth, but hastily picked himself up and hurried on as if nothing had happened.
> *Winston Churchill (1874-1965), on Stanley Baldwin*

Political power can produce wealth more easily than wealth can produce power.
> *A. Cobban (1901-1968)*

When there is no middle class, and the poor greatly exceed in number, troubles arise, and the state soon comes to an end.
> *Aristotle (384-322 BCE)*

If you cry "Forward!" you must without fail make plain in which direction to go.
> *Anton Chekhov (1860-1904)*
> *[and look back from time to time to see if they are still following. LZ)*

The real science of political economy, which has yet to be distinguished from the bastard science, as medicine from witchcraft, and astronomy from astrology, is that which teaches nations to desire and labor for the things that lead to life.
> *John Ruskin (1819-1900)*

Power is so apt to be insolent, and liberty so saucy, that they are very seldom upon good terms.
> *Marquis of Halifax (1633-1695)*

The people may be made to follow a course of action, but they may not be made to understand it.
> *Confucius (551-479 BCE)*

It is cheap generosity which promises the future in compensation for the present.
> *J. A. Soencer*

Nations are like men; they love that which flatters their passions even more than that which serves their interests.
> *Alexis de Tocqueville (1805-1859)*

I tremble for my country when I reflect that God is just.
> *Thomas Jefferson (1743-1826), in 1784, concerning wrongs done to the Indians*

The party system is arranged on the same principle as a three-legged race: the principle that union is not always strength and is never activity.
> *Gilbert Keith Chesterton (1874-1936)*

The state has learned from merchants and industrialists how to exploit credit; it defies the nation ever to let it go into bankruptcy. Alongside all swindlers the state now stands there as swindler-in-chief.
> *Jakob Burckhardt (1818-97)*

Who shall stand guard to the guards themselves?
> *Juvenal (60?-140?)*

Corruptio optimi pessima
The Corruption of the best is the worst of all.
> *Latin maxim*

Big thieves hang little ones.
> *Czech proverb*

Politics is the most miserable of human activities.
  Jorge Luis Borges (1899-1986)

An army of stags led by a lion is more to be feared than an army of lions
led by a stag.
  Chabrias (d. 357 BC ?), Athenian general

The two most important rules in Washington D.C. are:
Rule One: "The cover-up is worse than the event".
Rule Two: "No one ever remembers the first rule".
  Quoted by Donald Rumsfeld (1932-   )

The English people thinks it is free. It is gravely mistaken; it is free only
during parliamentary elections; as soon as the members are elected, the
people are enslaved.
  Jean-Jacques Rousseau (1712-1778)

Ideologies are the opium of the intellectuals.
  Raymond Aron
  [A play on Marx: "Religion is the opium of the people".LZ]

The introduction of religious passion into politics is the end of honest
politics, and the introduction of politics into religion is the prostitution of
true religion.
  Lord Halisham (1907-2001)

World peace begings with you.
  Bumper sticker

A nation is a society united by a delusion about its ancestry and by a
common hatred of its neighbors.
  Dean William R. Inge (1860-1954)

Power corrupts, but absolute power is really neat.

You can fool some of the people all of the time, and all of the people some
of the time. That usually is sufficient.

Taxation WITH representation is not so hot either.

Stop repeat offenders. Don't re-elect them!

Politicians and diapers have one thing in common: They should both be
changed regularly and for the same reason.

Don't steal. The government hates competition.

Annoy a politician today. THINK.

Don't ask what your country can do for you; ask your congressman.
> *Leon Zeldis*

POSITIVE THINKING

My friend thought he was not gonna make it. Then he started thinking positive. Now he's positive he's not gonna make it.
> *Sammy Shore*

The impossible always happens.
> *Talleyrand (1754-1838)*

We shall find a way, or we shall make it.
> *Hannibal (247?-183 BCE)*

If you are not criticized, you may not be doing much.
> *Donald Rumsfeld (1932-   )*

Life is to be lived, not controlled, and humanity is won by continuing to play in the face of certain defeat.
> *Ralph Ellison (1914-1994)*

Don't cry because it ended, smile because it happened.
> *Gabriel García Márquez (1928-   )*

Being defeated is often a temporary condition. Giving up is what makes it permanent.
> *Marlene vos Savant (1946-   )*

The pessimist complains about the wind;
The optimist expects it to change;
The realist adjusts the sails.
> *William Arthur Ward (1921-1997)*

One ship sails east, another west,
By the self-same winds that blow.
It isn't the gales, it's the set of the sails
That determines the way we go.
> *Ella Wheeler Wilcox (1850-1919)*

A person who smiles in the face of adversity... probably has a scapegoat.

Teamwork means never having to take all the blame yourself.

Indecision is the key to Flexibility.

POSSIBLE

The possible is limited; the impossible is immense.
> *Alphonse de Lamartine (1790-1869)*

The impossible takes longer.
> *Vera Weizmann (1881-1968), wife of Israel's first President*

PRAYER

Good deeds are the best prayer.
> *Serbian proverb*
> *(cf. the Spanish: 'A Dios rogando y con el mazo dando' – Pray to God and wield the hammer. LZ)*

As long as teachers give tests, prayer in schools will continue.

What men usually ask of God when they pray is that two and two not make four.

PREACHING

You can preach a better sermon with your life than with your lips.
> *Oliver Goldsmith (1728-1774)*

Preach the faith until you have it, then preach because you have it.
> *Friedrich Nietzsche (1844-1900)*

Preaching is like drilling for oil: if you haven't hit something in twenty minutes, it's time to quit boring.
> *[Ditto about after-dinner speakers. LZ]*

PREDICTIONS

Predictions are unreliable, particularly about the future.
> *Samuel Goldwin (1882-1974)*

Everything that can be invented, has been invented.
>*Charles H. Duell, Commissioner of the U.S. Patents Office, in 1899*

You must be calm before you can utter oracles.
>*Henry David Thoreau (1817-1862)*

The only way to predict the future is to have the power to shape the future.
>*Eric Hoffer (1902-1983)*

It doesn't pay to prophets to be too specific.
>*L. Sprague de Camp (1907-2000)*

The future smells of Russian leather, blood, godlessness, and many whippings. I should advice our grandchildren to be born with very thick skins on their backs.
>*Henrich Heine (1797-1856)*
>*[He wasn't much off the mark. Stalin took power in 1922, Hitler in 1933. LZ]*

I have suffered many things in my life, most of which never happened.
>*Mark Twain (Samuel Clemens) (1835-1910)*

When Gary Cooper turned down the Rhett Butler role in *Gone with the Wind*, he is said to have remarked "I'm just glad it will be Clark Gable who's falling flat on his face and not Gary Cooper".

X-rays will prove to be a hoax.
Heavier-than-air flying machines are impossible.
>*Lord Kelvin (1824-1907), British mathematician, physicist and President of the British Royal Society, c. 1883 and 1895, respectively.*

The Revd. Dionysius Lardner, Professor of Science at University College London, declared roundly at a public meeting in 1835 that "man has as much chance of crossing the Atlantic by steamship as going to the moon". Brunel proved him wrong in 1838, with 200 tons of coal to spare.
>*Trevor Fishlock*
>*[and the moon trip took only a little more than a century to become true. LZ)*

There is not the slightest indication that nuclear energy will ever be available.
>*Albert Einstein(1879-1955) in 1932. Later, of course, he changed his mind*

I think there is a world market for maybe five computers.
    Thomas Watson, Chairman of IBM, in 1943

Why don't you ever see the headline "Psychic wins Lottery"?]

In 1893, Sir Robert Bolt convinced the Royal Academy of Sciences that communication with the planet Mars was impossible, because the flag would have to be as large as Ireland, which would be impossible to move.

Some people keep predicting the end of the world in spite of the fact that they are always wrong. But it is admitted that they get a little nearer each time.

The future isn't what it used to be.

PRIDE

Half of the harm that is done in this world is due to people who want to feel important. They don't mean to do harm but the harm does not interest them.
    T. S. Eliot, poet (1888-1965)

They are proud in humility, proud in that they are not proud.
    Robert Burton (1577-1640)

I agree to be modest, on condition everybody knows about it.
    Victor Eftimiu (1889-1972)

He is a modest man who has a good deal to be modest about.
    Winston Churchill (1874-1965), about Clement Atlee

Those who get too big for their britches will be exposed in the end.

PRINCIPLES

It is easier to fight for one's principles than to live up to them.
    Alfred Adler (1870-1937)

If a fellow says 'It ain't the money, it's the principle', it's the money.
    Kin Hubbard (1968-1930)

A thing moderately good is not so good as it ought to be. Moderation in temper is always a virtue, but moderation in principle is always a vice.
    Thomas Paine (1737-1809)

These are my principles, and if you don't like them… well, I have others.
Groucho Marx (1890-1977)

Principles are strategy; politics, tactics.
Leon Zeldis

PRINTING

Printer's axiom: you can have it fast, cheap or accurate. Pick two.
[This is also called a trilemma. LZ]

Aldus Manutius the Elder (d. 1515) is credited with having printed the first semicolon, and also with inventing the italic face.

PRIZES

I don't deserve this award, but I have arthritis and I don't deserve that either.
Jack Benny (1894-1974)

What do Eucken and Spitteler have in common? They won the Nobel Prize for Literature. What do Franz Kafka and Aldous Huxley have in common? They never did.
Leon Zeldis

PROBLEMS

Each epoch has its problems, and by solving them Humanity advances further.
Heinrich Heine (1797-1856)

If we can really understand the problem, the answer will come out of it, because the answer is not separate from the problem.
J. Krishnamurti (1895-1986)

When solving problems, dig at the roots instead of just hacking at the leaves.
Anthony J. D'Angelo

Idealism increases in direct proportion to one's distance from the problem.
John Galsworthy (1867-1933)

For every human problem there is a neat, simple solution; and it is always wrong.
H. L. Mencken (1880-1956)

Inside every large problem is a small problem struggling to get out.

PROFESSIONALS

When I realized what I had turned out to be was a lousy, two-bit pool hustler and a drunk, I wasn't depressed at all. I was glad to have a profession.
Danny McGoorty, Irish pool player

The ark was built by amateurs; the Titanic was built by professionals.

PROGRESS

In our industry [Intel - computer chip manufacturer], we sell a memory chip with something like 66 or 67 million transistors for less than we sold an individual transistor for when I got into the business. It's really a 67 million-fold decrease in the cost of the product and you get all the interconnections free. But that doesn't show in the productivity figures.
Gordon Moore (1929), co-founder of Intel, writing in 2001

The new electronic independence recreates the world in the image of a global village.
Marshall McLuhan (1911-1980)

Man's mind, once stretched to a new idea, never regains its original dimensions.
Oliver Wendell Holmes, Jr. (1841-1935)

Routine is not organization, any more than paralysis is order.
Arthur Helps (1813-1875)

The most important discoveries will provide answers to questions that we do not yet know to ask and will concern objects that we have not yet imagined.
John N. Bahcall (1935-2005)

The rung of a ladder was never meant to rest upon, but only to hold a man's foot long enough to enable him to put the other somewhat higher.
Thomas Henry Huxley (1825-1895)

Through loyalty to the past, our mind refuses to realize that tomorrow's joy is possible only if today's makes way for it, that each wave owes the beauty of its line only to the withdrawal of the preceding one.
André Gide (1869-1951)

Never put off doing something useful for fear of evil that may never arrive.
James Watson (1928-)

Nothing in progression can rest on its original plan. We might as well think of rocking a grown man in the cradle of an infant.
Edmund Burke (1729-1797)

All rising to a great place is by a winding stair.
Francis Bacon (1561-1626)

Daring ideas are like chessmen moved forward; they may be beaten, but they may start a winning game.
Johann von Goethe (1749-1832)

Progress of scientific and technical knowledge is cumulative, but in art, literature and music, earlier work is never superseded. Major art is not relegated to antiquarian status. Chartres does not date.
George Steiner (1929-)

You can walk the path only after becoming the path itself.
H.P. Blavatsky (1831-1891)
[cf. the poet Machado's lines: Walker, there is no road; the road is made by walking]

We trained hard and, just when it appeared that we were prevailing, we were reorganized. What a wonderful method to give the illusion of progress, whilst totally demoralizing the troops.
Seneca (4 BCE-65 CE)

When white man colonized North America, Indians were running it. No taxes. No debt. Plenty buffalo. Plenty beaver. Medicine man free. Women did most of the work. Indian men hunted and fished all the time. White man dumb enough to think he could improve system like that.
Ramiro-Arteta Guzmán

Is it progress if a cannibal uses knife and fork?
Stanislaus Lec

The reasonable man adapts himself to the world; the unreasonable one persists in trying to adapt the world to himself. Therefore all progress depends on the unreasonable man.
George Bernard Shaw (1856-1950)

Life must be lived forwards, but can only be understood backwards.
Sören Kierkegaard (1813-1865)

It is not obligatory for a generation to have great men.
José Ortega y Gasset (1883-1955)

May you live in interesting times.
Chinese curse

In Italy, for thirty years under the Borgias, they had warfare, terror, murder and bloodshed, but they produced Michelangelo, Leonardo da Vinci, and the Renaissance. In Switzerland, they had brotherly love, they had five hundred years of democracy and peace - and what did they produce? The cockoo clock.
From the movie The Third Man, 1949

Behold the turtle. He makes progress only when he sticks his neck out.
James Bryan Conant (1893-1978)

In 1900... there were 7,000 horse-drawn cabs and 3,000 buses daily, totaling nearly 40,000 horses at work in London, each emitting 20 liters of solid effluent a day, or more than a quarter of a million tons a year... At least 25 percent of this, or 70,000 tons, was dropped in the street and had to be picked up, largely by hand. Mechanized transport reduced both the accident rate to human beings and cruelty to animals.
Henry Hobhouse (1854-1937)

PROJECTS

Plan ahead - it wasn't raining when Noah built the ark.
Howard Ruff (1931-)

Most projects start out slowly – and then sort of taper off.
Norman R. Augustine (1935-)

If you fail to plan, you plan to fail.

The six phases of a project:
1. Enthusiasm
2. Disillusionment
3. Panic
4. Search for the guilty
5. Punishment of the innocent
6. Praise and accolades for non-participants

PROMISES

'Mean to' don't pick no cotton.

I'll stop procrastinating tomorrow.

We make promises to the extent that we hope - and keep them to the extent that we fear.

I'm generous with promises; never keep them.
Leon Zeldis

PSYCHIATRY

Much will be gained if we succeed in transforming your hysterical misery into common unhappiness.
Sigmund Freud (1856-1939)

Sometimes a cigar is just a cigar.
Attributed to Sigmund Freund

Psychoanalysis is the way in which any person can be Jewish.
Nathan Adler

Psychoanalysis is essentially an art.
Françoise Davoine

Why all this fuss and bother about the mystery of the unconscious? What about the mystery of the conscious? What do they know about that?
James Joyce (1882-1941)

Recently the advanced researches of neurophsycoanalysis have been able to demonstrate that the Freudian supposition appears to be based on scientific reality. It seems that the fundamental drives of sexuality, of love,

of hate, of ambition, fear, daring and much more have roots in a primitive part of the brain that operates below the horizon of consciousness known as the limbic system.
James Lord

Psychoanalysis: the occupation of aroused rationalists who trace everything in the world to sexual causes with the exception of their occupation.
Karl Kraus (1874-1936)

The greatest discovery of Freud was that what appears to us as most arbitrary and most incomprehensible in the life of the spirit can be analyzed and understood rationally.
Claude Levi-Strauss (1908-   )

The relation between psychiatrists and other kinds of lunatics is the same as that between concave madnes and convex one.
Karl Kraus (1874-1936)

In California everyone goes to a therapist, is a therapist or is a therapist going to a therapist.
Truman Capote (1924-1984)

Anyone who goes to a psychiatrist ought to have his head examined.
Samuel Goldwyn (1882-1974)

A psychiatrist is a man who goes to the Follies-Bergere and looks at the audience.
Mervyn Stockwood

Behavioral psychology is the science of pulling habits out of rats.
Dr. Douglas Busch

All practicing psychiatrists can confirm the obvious proliferation of diagnosis of bipolar depression, to the point it has become a sociological fact, like hysteria was at the time when psychoanalysis flourished. As everybody was then hysteric, now we all are bipolar, or are likely to be diagnosed as such.
Marco Antonio de la Parra (1952-   )

Making a diagnosis involves whoever makes it, and not only the diagnosed person.
Marco Antonio de la Parra (1952-   )

Biology is the hardware and psychology the software.
    Quoted by Marco Antonio de la Parra (1952-   )

The superego is that part of the personality which is soluble in alcohol.
    Prof. Harold Lasswell (1902-1978)

Does the name Pavlov ring a bell?

There is a very fine line between "hobby" and "mental illness".

The neurotic builds castles in the air, the psychotic lives in them, and the psychoanalyst collects the rent.

PUBLIC

The public will believe anything so long as it is not founded on truth.
    Edith Sitwell (1887-1964)

The Hebrew word for the public is *Tsibur*, composed of the three consonants Ts, B and R, which are the initials for *Tsadik, Beinoni* and *Rashah*: Virtuous, Average and Evil person. The public is composed of all three kinds of people.

RACE

Race is nothing and language all; for the blood carries only physical resemblance, which is simple and very individual; while the word carries thought, custom, law and prejudice, which are complex and universal.
    Vernon Lee (1856-1935)

RADIOACTIVITY

Radioactive cats have 18 half-lives.
    Randy K. Builder

REASON

Reason is our contact with the Most High.
    Maimonides (Moses ben Maimon) (1135-1204)

On the contrary to all specialized arts, all sciences together are only human intelligence, which remains the same, no matter to what object is applied. Thus, the main benefit man can obtain is to increase the natural light of his reason, not to solve this or that problem, but so that in all

circumstances of life, his understanding shows to his will what must be chosen.
> *René Descartes (1596-1650)*

There are two kinds of madness: excluding reasons and admitting only reason.
> *Blaisé Pascal (1623-1662)*

We have a tendency not to reason, but to mystery; not to the penetrating and clear thought, but to sorcery; not to the human intellect searching for explanation but to the gnostic omniscience in the absurd; not to science but to sorcery behind scientific masks; not to activity founded on reasoning, but on magic.
> *Karl Jaspers (1883-1969)*

Our prejudices are our mistresses; reason is at best our wife, very often needed, but seldom minded.
> *Earl of Chesterfield (1694-1773)*

There is quite a lot of evidence to show that humans are not very good at using idealized forms of rationality, such as logical deduction. Asked whether a conclusion flows from a given premise, most people are likely to accept as valid an invalid conclusion if it happens to be consistent with their own beliefs.
> *Paul Crichton*

Christian theology is not only opposed to the scientific spirit; it is opposed to every other form of rational thinking.
> *H. L. Mencken (1880-1956)*

REDUNDANCY

Help stamp out and abolish redundancy.
> *Terri Hammers*

REGRETS

Three things they say come not back to men nor women: the spoken word, the past life, and the neglected opportunity.
> *J. M. Barrie (1860-1937)*

No one is rich enough to buy back his past.
> *Oscar Wilde (1854-1900)*

Regret for the things we did can be tempered by time; it is regret for the things we did not do that is inconsolable.
Sydney J. Harris (1917-1986)

Footfalls echo in the memory
Down the passage which we did not take
Towards the door we never opened
Into the rose-garden.
T. S. Eliot (1888-1965)

Look in my face; my name is Might-have-been
I am also called No-more, Too-late, Farewell...
Dante Gabriel Rosetti (1828-1882)

The trouble with life is that there are so many beautiful women and so little time.
John Barrymore (1882-1942)

Nothing is as good as it seems beforehand.
George Eliot (1819-1880)

RELIGION

What today is atheism, tomorrow will be religion.
Ludwig Feuerbach (1804-1872)

Religion is a disease, but it is a noble disease.
Heraclitus (6th-5th c. BCE)

We have just enough religion to make us hate, but not enough to make us love one another.
Jonathan Swift (1667-1745)

The last Christian died on the cross.
Friedrich Nietzsche (1844-1900)

The Churches must learn humility as well as teach it.
George Bernard Shaw (1856-1950)

Fears are the price of religious hope.
Roy Porter (1946-2002)

The gaming table can be as effective a means of grace as the Communion table.
John Bigelow (1817-1911)

As far as I can remember, there is not one word in the Gospels in praise of intelligence.
Bertrand Russell (1872-1970)

Every religion begins in spirituality and becomes extint in materialism.
Frédéric Portal (1804-1876)

We cannot know whether we love God, although there may be strong reasons for thinking so, but there can be no doubt about whether we love our neighbor or not.
Saint Theresa (1515-1582)

The creation was an act of mercy.
William Blake (1757-1827)

Faith heightens guilt, it does not prevent sin.
Cardinal John Henry Newman (1801-1890)

The confessional box only appeared during the sixteenth century.
Jacques le Goff (1924-   )

Superstition is rooted in a much deeper and more sensitive layer of the psyche than skepticism.
Johann von Goethe (1749-1832)

Human nature was stained by original sin and is therefore more disposed to vice than to virtue.
Pope Leo XIII (1810-1903)

Men never do evil so completely and cheerfully as when they do it from religious conviction.
Blaise Pascal (1623-1662)

The introduction of religious passion into politics is the end of honest politics, and the introduction of politics into religion is the prostitution of true religion.
Lord Halisham (1907-2001)

Political freedom cannot exist in any land where religion controls the state, and religious freedom cannot exist in any land where the state controls religion.
Samuel James Ervin Jr. (1896-1985)

Religion is the masterpiece of the art of animal training, for it trains people as to how they shall think.
Schopenhauer (1788-1860)

The various modes of worship which prevailed in the Roman world were all considered by the people as equally true; by the philosopher as equally false; and by the magistrate as equally useful.
Edward Gibbon (1737-1794)

Leopards break into the temple and drink the sacrificial chalices dry; this occurs repeatedly, again and again; finally, it can be reckoned upon beforehand and becomes part of the ceremony.
Franz Kafka (1883-1924)

We have just enough religion to make us hate, but not enough to make us love one another.
Jonathan Swift (1667-1745)

Most men's anger about religion is as if two men should quarrel for a lady that neither of them care for.
Marquis of Halifax (1633-1695)

The question turns mainly on whether the strange Greek in which the four Gospels are written in simply the work of Jews thinking in Aramaic though writing in Greek, or whether it represents rather an effort to translate literally into Greek original Aramaic Gospels now lost.
Ernest Sutherland Bates (1879-1939)
[But the Dead Sea manuscripts prove that Hebrew was at that time the preferred language for writing among Jews. LZ]

It ain't the parts of the Bible that I can't understand that bother me, it's the parts that I do understand.
Mark Twain (1835-1910)

So many gods, so many creeds,
so many paths that wind and wind,
while just the art of being kind
is all the sad world needs.
Ella Wheeler Wilcoxt (1850-1919)

I won't take my religion from any man who never works except with his mouth.
> *Carl Sandburg (1878-1967)*

It is customary to blame secular science and anti-religious philosophy for the eclipse of religion in modern society. It would be more honest to blame religion for its own defeats. Religion declined not because it was refuted but because it became irrelevant, dull, oppressive and insipid. When faith is completely replaced by creed, worship by discipline, love by habit; when the crisis of today is ignored because of the splendor of the past; when faith becomes an heirloom rather than a living fountain; when religion speaks only in the name of authority rather than with the voice of compassion, its message becomes meaningless... The primary task of philosophy of religion is to rediscover the questions to which religion is an answer. In our quest for forgotten questions, the method and spirit of philosophical inquiry are of greater importance than theology. Theology starts with dogma, philosophy begins with problems. Philosophy sees the problem first, theology has the answer in advance.
> *Rabbi Abraham Joshua Heschel (1907-1972)*

Compulsion in religion is distinguished peculiarly from compulsion in every other thing. I may grow rich by an art I am compelled to follow; I may recover health by medicines I am compelled to take against my own judgment, but I cannot be saved by a worship I disbelieve and abhor.
> *Thomas Jefferson (1743-1826)*

There is a goal, but no way; what we call the way is mere wavering.
> *Franz Kafka (1883-1924)*

The climax of Galileo's trial came in 1633, when the Holy Office found him "vehemently suspected of heresy, that is, of having held and believed that the sun is the center of the world and is immovable". Galileo's *Dialogue on the Two Chief World-Systems* was removed from the Index of Prohibitted Books only in 1835.

What men usually ask of God when they pray is that two and two not make four.

Give me some of that old-time Religion. Ave Jupiter!

Billboard: Jesus Saves. Someone added: But Moses invests!

Sects, sects, sects. Is that all you monks ever think about?

On the sixth day God created the platypus; and God said: "Let's see the evolutionists figure this one out."

Religion demands skepticism to blossom, the same as a flower needs the sun. Too large a dose kills both.
> *Leon Zeldis*

A new religion is created in America every 50 years or less.
> *Leon Zeldis*

REST

There is no rest for free peoples. Rest is a monarchic idea.
> *George Clemenceau (1841-1929)*

REVOLUTION

Revolution starts as promise, is dissipated in frenetic agitation and congeals into bloody dictatorships. In all revolutionary movements, the sacred time of myth is inexorably transformed into the profane time of history.
> *Octavio Paz (1914-1998)*

Revolution begins by the word and ends by the sword.
> *Jean Paul Marat (1743-1793)*

Every successful revolution puts on in time the robes of the tyrant it has deposed.
> *Barbara Tuchman (1912-1989)*
> *[Recent examples: Russia, China, Cuba. LZ]*

Whoever trembles is guilty.
> *Maximilien de Roberpierre (1758-1794)*

The purity of a revolution can last a fortnight.
> *Jean Cocteau (1891-1963)*

Men who use terrorism as a means to power, rule by terror once they are in power.
> *Helen MacInnes (1907-1985)*

RICHES

Riches should come as the reward for hard work, preferably one's forebears.
> *Sir Steven Runciman (1903-2000)*

Give me the luxuries of life and I will willingly do without the necessities.
> *Frank Lloyd Wright (1869-1959)*

With the greater part of rich people, the chief enjoyment of riches consists in the parade of riches.
> *Adam Smith (1723-1790)*

The rich are considered to be bad, insolent, inhumane, while the poor are humble, courageous, charitable. So why all the people want to be rich?
> *Marcel Colucci*

To suppose, as we all do, that we could be rich and not behave the way the rich behave, is like supposing that we could drink all day and stay sober.
> *Logan Pearsall Smith (1865-1946)*

Wealth is like a viper, which is harmless if a man knows how to take hold of it; but if he does not, it will twist around his hand and bite him.
> *St. Clement (1ˢᵗ c.)*

Behind every great fortune there is a crime.
> *Honoré de Balzac (1799-1850)*

No one can earn a million dollars honestly.
> *William Jennings Bryan (1860-1925)*

As a general rule, nobody has the money he deserves.
> *Benjamin Disraeli (1804-1881)*

If the rich could hire other people to die for them, the poor could make a wonderful living.
> *Yiddish proverb*

It doesn't matter if you're rich or poor, as long as you've got money.
> *Joe E. Lewis (1902-1971)*

Being rich is having money, being wealthy is having time.
> *Margaret Bonnano*

It isn't necessary to be rich and famous to be happy. It's only necessary to be rich.
> *Alan Alda (1936-   )*

Better to be nouveau than never to have been riche at all.

It's not hard to meet expenses; they are everywhere.

RIPOSTES

Heckler: "Mr. Churchill, you are drunk!"
Churchill: "Yes, I am; and you are ugly. But tomorrow I shall be sober."
I am enclosing two tickets for the first night of my new play. Bring a friend...if you have one.
> *George Bernard Shaw to Winston Churchill, who replied:*
> Cannot possibly attend first night, will attend second... if there is one.

RUSSIA

I cannot forecast the action of Russia. It is a riddle wrapped in a mystery inside an enigma.
> *Winston Churchill (1874-1965)*

If Lenin's widow does not behave, we will appoint someone else as Lenin's widow.
> *Josef Stalin (1879-1953)*

We Russians don't know how to live like saints, we only know how to die like saints.
> *Vasily Grossman (1906-1964)*

Against bodies, violence; against souls, lies.
> *The ruling principle of Serge Netchayev (1847-1882), Russian revolutionary disciple of Bakunin, mentor of Lenin*

Russia: heavy, chilling history, savagery, bureaucracy, poverty and ignorance.
> *Anton Chekhov (1860-1904)*

Despotism tempered by assassination - that is our Magna Charta.
> *Annonymous Russian*

St. Petersburg represents real barbarism, barely disguised under a revolting magnificence.
> *Marquis de Custine (1790-1857), visiting the city in 1839*

St. Petersburg is Russian, but it is not Russia.
> *Czar Nicholas I (1796-1855), host of the Marquis de Custine*

Russia is the subconscious of the West.
> *Anthony Burgess (1917-1993)*

What do you call a Soviet orchestra that's been touring in the West? A string trio.
> *Russian joke during the Stalin era*

SACRIFICE

Self-sacrifice enables us to sacrifice other people without blushing.
> *George Bernard Shaw (1856-1950)*

SAFETY

The desire for safety stands guard against every great and noble enterprise.
> *Publius Cornelius Tacitus (55?-118?)*

SAINTS

Saints should always be judged guilty before they are proved innocent.
> *George Orwell (1903-1950)*

Every saint has a past, and every sinner has a future.
> *Oscar Wilde (1854-1900)*

Saint: A dead sinner revised and edited.
> *Ambrose Bierce (1842-1914)*

SCHOLARSHIP

Junk is junk, but the history of junk is scholarship.
> *Burton Dreben*

The Golden Rule of academic research: those with the gold make the rules.

What nature didn't give, the university will not lend.
Spanish proverb

SCIENCE

The word science had different connotations in the past. At the beginning of the nineteenth century, it stood for any organized body of knowledge; chemistry, history and theology were all sciences in this sense, whereas engineering was described as an art. Snow's gulf between the two cultures did not exist.
Judith Hawley

It would be possible to describe everything scientifically, but it would make no sense; it would be without meaning, as if you described a Beethoven symphony as a variation of wave pressure.
Albert Einstein (1879-1955)

It is surely one of the curious paradoxes of history that science, which professionally has little to do with faith, owes its origins to an act of faith, that the universe can be rationally interpreted, and that science today is sustained by that assumption.
Loren C. Eiseley (1907-1977)

If the facts don't fit the theory, change the facts.
Attributed to Albert Einstein (1879-1955)

If I have ever made any valuable discoveries, it has been owing more to patient attention than to any other talent.
Sir Isaac Newton (1642-1727)

I have no particular talent; I am merely extremely inquisitive.
Albert Einstein (1879-1955)

It is the theory that decides what we can observe.
Albert Einstein (1879-1955), told in 1925 to the young Werner Heisenberg (1901-1976)

Science is an attempt to make the chaotic diversity of our sense-experience correspond to a logically uniform system of thought.
Albert Einstein (1879-1955)

No amount of experimentation can ever prove me right; a single experiment can prove me wrong.
Albert Einstein (1879-1955)

Testing can prove the presence of errors, but not their absence.
    Edgar Dijkstra (1930-2002)

If you torture data sufficiently, it will confess to almost anything.
    Fred Menge (1937-   )

Scientists are specialized barbarians who... tend to live in a perpetual present with no respect for the past and little interest in the future.
    José Ortega y Gasset (1883-1955)

We must be clear that, when it comes to atoms, language can be used only as in poetry.
    Niels Bohr (1885-1962)

We live in a universe whose age we can't quite compute, surrounded by stars whose distance from us and each other we don't know, filled with matter we can't identify, operating in conformance with physical laws whose propertiers we don't truly understand.
    Bill Bryson (1951-   )

The most exciting phrase to hear in science, the one that heralds the most discoveries, is not "Eureka!" (I found it!) but "That's funny".
    Isaac Asimov (1920-1992)

Knowledge that is not being used for the winning of further knowledge does not even remain – it decays and disappears.
    J. D. Bernal (1901-1971)

True science teaches, above all, to doubt and to be ignorant.
    Miguel de Unamuno (1864-1936)

Every great advance in natural knowledge [*i.e. scientific knowledge*] has involved the absolute rejection of authority.
    T. H. Huxley (1825-1895)

Blinded by what can be called the "scientistic prejudice", Philosophy, believing thus to be able to reach the status of science, becomes pure calculation, a mere play with what is humanly indifferent, an algorithm operating only with logical-mathematical concepts, an axiomatics without objective meaning.
    Martin Heidegger (1889-1976)

The scientific ideal has become the target of all knowledge and the only legitimate means of accessing reality.
    Martin Heidegger (1889-1976)

What is most prized in science, and is most profound, is the discovery of a vast absence of knowledge, of a range of hitherto undiscovered truths, owing to the breakdown of a standard model.
Gerald Holton

Science is rooted in conversations.
Werner Heisenberg (1901-1976)

What is now proved was once only imagined.
William Blake (1757-1827)

Any sufficiently advanced technology is indistinguishable from magic.
Arthur C. Clark (1917-   )

Scientists have become the alchemists of our time, working in secret ways which cannot be divulged, casting spells which embrace us all.
Solly Zuckerman (1904-1993)

The dangers threatening modern science cannot be averted by more experimenting, for our complicated experiments have no longer anything to do with nature in her own right, but with nature changed and transformed by our own cognitive activity.
Werner Heisenberg (1901-1976)

To be rational or scientific is only one among virtues; no sane man would pretend that it is the whole of virtue.
Bertrand Russell (1872-1970)

Scientific theories are heading towards the truth.
Lawrence Sklar

Often a subject that has been regarded for centuries as part of philosophy becomes emancipated and acquires an independent status. This happened long ago to physics, which is still known in the titles of the older university chairs as "Natural Philosophy", and it has happened within living memory to psychology and to logic.
Edmund Whittaker (1873-1956)

The great tragedy of science: the slaying of a beautiful hypothesis by an ugly fact.
Thomas Huxley (1825-1895)

Although this may seem a paradox, all exact science is dominated by the idea of approximation.
Bertrand Russell (1872-1970)

Art is I, science is we.
Claude Bernard (1813-1878)

Since historians know as little about science as scientists know about history, the historian of science can easily keep out of reach of experts in either camp.
James R. Newman (1907-1966)

Science is built of facts just as houses are built of bricks; but an accumulation of facts is no more science that a pile of bricks is a house.
Henri Poincaré (1854-1912)

Science and technology, unlike literature, art, music and philosophy, do not attain the condition of timelessness: a nineteenth-century steam engine is now a historical curio. A novel by Dostoevsky is not.
George Steiner (1929-   )

A new scientific truth does not triumph by convincing its opponents and making them see the light, but rather because its opponents eventually die, and a new generation grows up that is familiar with it.
Max Planck (1858-1947)

You see what you know, or what you believe that you know.
Johann von Goethe (1749-1832)

Don't worry if your theory doesn't agree with the observations, because they are probably wrong.
Sir Arthur Eddington (1882-1944)

The Atoms of Democritus
And Newton's Particles of light
Are sands upon the Red Sea shore
Where Israel's tents do shine so bright.
William Blake (1757-1827)

Scientists are Peeping Toms at the keyhole of eternity.
Arthur Koestler (1905-1983)

It was recently discovered that research causes cancer in rats.

All otherwise inexplicable phenomena of science can be explained by magic.

SECURITY

Security is mostly a superstition. It does not exist in nature, nor do the children of men as a whole experience it. Avoiding danger is no safer in the long run than outright exposure. Life is a daring adventure or nothing at all.
 Helen Keller (1880-1968)

It is much more secure to be feared than to be loved.
 Niccolo Machiavelli (1469-1527)

SELF-CRITICISM

I have offended God and mankind because my work didn't reach the quality it should have.
 Leonardo da Vinci (1452-1519)

My life has been nothing but a failure.
 Claude Monet (1840-1926)

It is harder to defeat oneself than one's enemies.
 Seneca (4 BCE- 65 CE)

SELF-IMPROVEMENT

Be faithful to that which exists nowhere but in yourself - and thus make yourself indispensable.
 André Gide (1869-1951)

We have to build a better man before we can build a better society.
 Paul Tillich (1886-1965)

There are times when a man should be content with what he has but never with what he is.
 William George Jordan (1864-1928)

He who asks of life nothing but the improvement of his own nature... is less liable than anyone else to miss and waste life.
 Henri Frédéric Amiel (1821-1881)

Never forget that you are unique, like everyone else.

Sociobiology...suggested that the biological process of self-improvement, which is going on all the time and is a vital element of human progress, should be studied by empirical science, not metaphysics, and by the methodology so brilliantly categorized by Karl Popper, in which theory is made narrow, specific and falsifiable by empirical data, as opposed to the all-purpose, untestable and self-modifying explanations of Marx, Freud, Levi-Strauss, Lacan, Barthes and other prophets.
Alexander Pope's conclusion: 'The proper study of mankind is man'.

The Three R's: Respect yourself, Respect the others, Responsibility in all your actions.

Improving the world is beyond the powers of most men, but improving oneself, anyone can do.
Leon Zeldis

The key to self-improvement is self-respect. When you realize you are the most important person in your life, you will try to make this a better person.
Leon Zeldis

SEX

The Abasid Caliph Mutawwakil slept with all 4,000 of his concubines in the 5,000 days of his reign.
Hugh Kennedy

Women need a reason to have sex. Men just need a place.
Billy Crystal (1948-)

There is more differences within the sexes than between them.
Ivy Comptom-Burnett (1884-1969)

In the sex-war thoughtlessness is the weapon of the male, vindictiveness of the female.
Cyril Connolly (1903-1974)

The trouble is that sex is a force of nature, and reason is not.
Ashley Brilliant (1933-)

SHADOWS

In India, if the shadow of an untouchable glances the body of a Brahmin, he must purify himself.

In China, you must not let your own shadow slip into an open casket or a grave. If it does, you'll die soon after.

Leonardo da Vinci intended to write a 'Book of the Shadows' in 1490. Only the table of contents has remained. He intended to describe the shadows as active beings, being capable of throwing "rays of darkness".
Esteban Cabezas

Noon is the hour when the sun swallows its own shadow, as fire swallows a straw.
Al-Biruni (d. 1050)

SILENCE

About which one cannot speak, one must keep silent.
Ludwig Wittgenstein (1889-1951)

Of those who say nothing, few are silent.
Thomas Neill (1850-1892)

Silence is not always a sign of wisdom, but babbling is ever a mark of folly.
Benjamin Franklin (1706-1790)

I like not only to be loved, but to be told that I am loved; the realm of silence is long enough beyond the grave.
George Eliot (Mary Ann Evans) (1819-1880)

Sometimes to remain silent is to lie.
Miguel de Unamuno (1864-1936)

Never miss a good chance to shut up.
Will Rogers (1879-1935)

Words are of time, silence is of eternity.
Thomas Carlyle (1795-1881)

Men were our Masters to teach us to speak, but we learn silence form the gods, from these we learn to hold our peace in their rites and ceremonies.
Plutarch (46?-120? CE)

Like a crazed locust, the cellular phone eats up what is left of silence.
George Steiner (1929-   )

Silences have a climax, when you have got to speak.
Elizabeth Bowen (1899-1973)

Human affairs would be far happier if the power in men to be silent were the same as that to speak. But... men govern nothing with more difficulty than their tongues.
Baruch Spinoza (1632-1677)

Not every truth is the better for showing its face undisguised; and often silence is the wisest thing for a man to heed.
Pindar (522-443 BCE)

Empty yourself of everything.
Let your mind rest at peace.
All things rise and fall
while the self watches their return.
They grow and flourish
and then return to the source.
Returning to the source is stillness,
which is the way of nature.
Tao Te Ching 16

There are two ends of the pole of silence. There is dead silence... which doesn't help any of us, and then there is the other silence, which is the supreme moment of communication - the moment when people normally divided from one another by every sort of natural human barrier suddenly find themselves truly together.
Peter Brook (1925-   )

He had occasional flashes of silence, that made his conversation perfectly delightful.
Sydney Smith (1771-1845) on Macaulay

Better to be silent and appear to be a fool, than to speak out and dispel all doubt.

Silence, like space, is infinite but, like space with bodies, only filling it with sound gives it meaning.
Leon Zeldis

SINGING

Anything that is too stupid to be spoken is sung.
Voltaire (1694-1778)

How wonderful opera would be if there were no singers.
Gioacchino Rossini (1792-1868)

He often broke into song because he couldn't find the key.

SINS

Hatred, envy, malice, jealousy and fear all have children. Any bad thought breeds others, and each of these goes on and on, ever repeating until our world is peopled with their offspring.
Ralph W. Trine

That which we call sin in others is experiment for us.
Ralph W. Emerson (1803-1882)

Other sins find their vent in the accomplishment of evil deeds, whereas pride lies in wait for good deeds to destroy them.
Saint Augustine (354-430)

When temptation knocks, imagination usually answers.
Dan Bennett

Lead us not into temptation. Just tells us where it is; we'll find it.
Sam Levenson (1911-1980)

The fifteenth century painted its virtues but described its sins.
Jan Huizinga

The wages of sin are unreported.

Until 1533, sodomy was not a crime in Common Law in England. Only the Act for the Punishment of the Vice of Buggery of 1533-34 made it a capital offence.

SLANDER

Rabbi Jochanan quoted a saying of Rabbi Simeon bar Yohai that injurious words constitute a greater wrong than monetary injury. The former affect a man's person, the other his profits. Financial harm can be repaired, but personal harm cannot.
Talmud, Baba Metzia, 58b

SLAVERY

About nineteen out of every twenty individuals have a 'natural and inalienable right' to be taken care of and protected, to have guardians, trustees, husbands, or masters; in other words, they have a natural and inalienable right to be slaves.
George Fitzhugh (1806-1881)

Men with immoderate mind can never be free; their passions forge their chains.
Edmund Burke (1729-1797)

By 1820, at least ten million African slaves had arrived in the New World, as opposed to a grand total of two million Europeans.
David Brion David

Rabbi Akiva ben Joseph was asked what kind of sinners would not obtain the Creator's pardon, and he answered: those who repent too much and those who sin intending to repent.

SLEEP

Sleep, riches and health, to be truly enjoyed, must be interrupted.
Johann Richter (1517-1616)

I don't care how smart a man is, he can't learn anything when he's asleep.
Bernard F. Gimbel (1885-1966)

Great eaters and great sleepers are incapable of anything else that is great.
Henri IV of France (1553-1610)

Plato condemns excessive sleep more than excessive drinking.
Michel de Montaigne (1533-1592)

Until the seventeenth century most Europeans spread bedding on the bare floor or on rushes.

SNOBBERY

Ladies and gentlemen are permitted to have friends in the kennel, but not in the kitchen.
> *George Bernard Shaw (1856-1950)*

Questioning is not the mode of conversation among gentlemen.
> *Dr. Samuel Johnson (1709-1784)*

Mr. Cobb took me into his library and showed me his books, of which he has a complete set.
> *Ring Lardner (1885-1933)*

SOCIOLOGY

No matter how many communes anybody invents, the family always creeps back.
> *Margaret Mead (1901-1978)*
> *[Look at the evolution of the kibbutz!, LZ]*

As human beings, we are constantly linked to universal life, and the simple viobration of an insect's antenna resounds in the infinity of the cosmos.
> *Amado Nervo (1870-1919)*

Society cannot exist unless a controlling power upon the will and appetite is placed somewhere; and the less of it there is within, the more must be without.
> *Edmund Burke (1729-1797)*

"If you are a good economist, a virtuous economist, you are reborn as a physicist," an Indian economist once said. "But if you are an evil, wicked economist, you are reborn as a sociologist".
> *Philip Ball (1962-   )*

It is no measure of health to be well adjusted to a profoundly sick society.
> *Krishnamurti (1895-1986)*

The classes that wash the most are those that work the least.
G. K. Chesterton (1874-1936)

SOLITUDE

Solitude is dangerous to reason, without being favorable to virtue.
Dr. Samuel Johnson (1709-1784)

Solitude! One word, so easy to pronounce, so endlessly hard to bear.
Adelbert von Chamisso (1781-1838)

One can acquire everything in solitude except character.
Stendhal (1783-1842)

Solitude: a good place to visit, but a poor place to stay.
Josh Billings (1818-1885)

SORROW

The first pressure of sorrow crushes out from our hearts the best wine;
afterwards the constant weight of it brings forth bitterness - the taste and
stain from the lees of the vat.
Henry Wardsworth Longfellow (1807-1882)

When sorrows come, they come not as single spies
But in battalions.
William Shakespeare (1564-1616)

A feeling of sadness and longing
That is not akin to pain,
And resembles sorrow only
As the mist resembles rain.
Longfellow (1807-1882)

There is no greater sorrow than to remember, in misery, the days when
we were happy.
Dante Alighieri (1265-1321)

When the trees in the forest see the ax they say: the wood of the handle is
of ours

SPAIN

Spain: cornerstone of all regions of the world.
Pablo Neruda (1904-1973)

Spanish is Latin as spoken by the Basque.
Miguel de Unamuno (1864-1936), Spanish (Basque) philosopher

In Spain, of every ten heads, nine rush forward and one thinks.
Antonio Machado (1875-1939)

Within fifty years of Columbus's arrival in the New World, the native population of Hispaniola had fallen from around 500,000 to less than 500. Within a century of the Europeans' arrival, roughly 90 percent of the population of the Americas perished.
David Brion Davis

SPEAKER

The right to be heard does not automatically include the right to be taken seriously.
Hubert H. Humphrey (1911-1978)

I take the view, and always have, that if you cannot say what you are going to say in twenty minutes, you ought to go away and write a book about it.
Lord Brabazon (1884-1964)

What orators lack in depth they make up in length

SPECULATION

To speculate without facts is to attempt to enter a house of which one has not the key, by wandering aimlessly round and round, searching the walls and now and then peeping through the windows. Facts are the key.
Julian Huxley (1887-1975)

There is a lot of uncertainty that's not clear in my mind
Gib Lewis, Texas House Speaker

STATISTICS

With most things, the average is mediocrity. With decision making, it's often excellence. You could say it's as if we've been programmed to be collectively smart.
>   *James Surowiecki (1967-   )*

Latest survey shows that 3 out of 4 people make up 75% of the world's population.

Remember that half the people you know are below average.

The 50-50-90 rule: Anytime you have a 50-50 chance of getting something right, there's a 90% probability you'll get it wrong.

There are lies, damn lies, and statistics.

STONE

One of the secrets of life is making stepping stones out of stumbling blocks.
>   *Jack Penn (1925-   )*

The oldest stone in Chile is found in the town of Belén (Bethlehem). It has been dated to 1,000 million years old.

Some peoples believed that stones mature within the earth. The ripest stone was diamond.
>   *Leon Zeldis*

STRUCTURE

A structure is a system that remains identical through transformations.
>   *Claude Levi-Strauss (1908-   )*

STUPIDITY

To succeed in the world it is not enough to be stupid, you must also be well-mannered.
>   *Voltaire (1694-1778)*

The first Rule of Holes is that when you are in one, you should stop digging. To keep right on doing what is already causing disastrous consequences is either insane or profoundly stupid.
    Molly Ivins (1944-2007)

Health nuts are going to feel stupid some day, lying in hospital dying of nothing.
    Redd Foxx (1922-1991)

SUCCESS

It is not enough to succeed, one's friends must fail.
    La Rochefoucauld (1613-1680)

The common idea that success spoils people by making them vain, egotistic and self-complacent is erroneous; on the contrary, it makes them, for the most part, humble, tolerant, and kind. Failure makes people cruel and bitter.
    Somerset Maugham (1874-1965)

Back of every achievement is a proud wife and a surprised mother-in-law.
    Brooks Hays (1898-1981)

Be like a postage stamp. Stick to one thing until you get there.
    Josh Billings (1818-1885)

To succeed in the world it is not enough to be stupid, you must also be well-mannered.
    Voltaire (1694-1778)

All successful men have agreed in one thing – they were causationists. They believed that things went not by luck, but by law; that there was not a weak or a cracked link in the chain that joins the first and last of things.
    Ralph Waldo Emerson (1803-1882)

Success comes in cans, failure in can'ts.
    Joel Weldon

SUICIDE

Without the possibility of suicide, I would have killed myself long ago.
    E. Michel Cioran (1911-1995)

SUPERSTITION

Superstition brings bad luck.
> *Umberto Eco (1932-   )*

I die worshipping God, loving my friends, not hating my enemies, detesting superstition.
> *Voltaire (1694-1778), just before dying*

Some 80 percent of Americans say they believe in angels.
> *T. M. Luhrmann (1962-   )*

Superstition is rooted in a much deeper and more sensitive layer of the psyche than skepticism.
> *Johann von Goethe (1749-1832)*

As students of nature we are pantheists, as poets polytheists, as moral beings monotheists.
> *Johann von Goethe (1749-1832)*

Some people still believe in Astrology, despite the evident fact that twins often have completely different destinies.
> *Leon Zeldis*

SWORDS

He who wants to draw the sword is a beginner. He who can draw the sword is an expert. He who is the sword is a master.
> *Risuke Otake (1926-   )*

Swords, like ships and buildings, have a soul. That's why they have names, like Excalubur, Tizona, etc.
> *Leon Zeldis*

SYMBOL

Beauty is symbol.
> *Plotinus (206?-270)*

Rituals are no more than symbols in action.
> *Comte de Larmandie (1798-1857)*

Language is to intelligence like symbols to intuition.
> *Dion Fortune (1890-1946)*

Images are the human mind's most eloquent, pregnant way of thinking. But they are hard to pin down in words.
>*David Gelernter*

It is through symbol that man, consciously or unconsciously, lives, works and has his being; those ages are accounted noblest which can best recognize symbolical worth, and prize it the highest.
>*Thomas Carlyle (1795-1881)*

If we can define allegory as the representation of something that can be expressed by another expressible thing, the mystical symbol is the expressible representation of something found beyond the sphere of expression and of communication, something that comes from a sphere where the face, so to say, is turned inwards and outside of us [....] the symbol does not "mean" anything and does not communicate anything, but makes transparent something that is outside of all expression.
>*Gershon Sholem (1897-1982)*

TACT

A wise man sees as much as he ought, not as much as he can.
>*Montaigne (1533-1592)*

Tact: Tongue in check.
>*Sue Dytri*

Tact is the intelligence of the heart.

Tact is going into a bathroom, finding a naked woman and retiring saying "Excuse me, Sir".

Tact is the result not of reading, but of breeding.
>*Leon Zeldis*

TAXES

We content that for a nation to try to tax itself into prosperity is like a man standing in a bucket and trying to lift himself up by the handle.
>*Sir Winston Churchill (1874-1965)*

The art of taxation consists in so plucking the goose as to get the most feathers with the least hissing.
>*Attributed to Colbert (1619-1683)*

The only difference between a taxman and a taxidermist is that the taxidermist leaves the skin.
Mark Twain (1835-1910)

Taxation WITH representation isn't so hot either.

The wages of sin are unreported.

TEACHING

To teach is to learn twice.
Joseph Joubert (1754-1824)

I play with all my best effort during lessons. This is the only way. Words are not enough. I do not believe in teachers who can only talk.
Pablo Casals (1876-1973)

The mediocre teacher tells. The good teacher explains. The superior teacher demonstrates. The great teacher inspires.
William Arthur Ward (1921-1997)

A teacher affects eternity; no one can tell where his influence stops.
Henry Adams (1838-1918)

As long as teachers give tests, prayer in schools will continue.

TECHNOLOGY

Any sufficiently advanced technology is indistinguishable from magic.
Arthur C. Clarke (1917-2008)

TELEVISION

Television is a medium so called because it is neither rare nor well done.
Ernie Kovacs (1919-1962)

Television is chewing gum for the eyes.
John Mason Brown (1900-1969)
[Also attributed to Frank Lloyd Wright]

Getting an award from TV is like getting kissed by someone with bad breath.
Mason Williams

There is a road from the eye to the heart that does not go through the intellect.
> *G.K. Chesterton (1874-1936)*
> *[written before the advent of television, yet so apposite. LZ]*

Soap operas wash out your brain.
> *Leon Zeldis*

Television: where a few words are worth a thousand pictures.
> *Leon Zeldis*

TEMPLE

One who does not rebuild the Temple in his generation is regarded as if he had destroyed it.
> *The Talmud*

The first step in the physical construction of the Temple is to rebuild our relationships with one another, and improve our attitude towards those who walk different paths than our own. When we can do that, our Sages promise, the tears we cry on Tisha Be'av [a day of mourning] will be tears of joy.
> *Jewish teaching*

TEXTILES

Impressed by a sign on the back of a truck: "If you can read this you're too darn close", a Houston lady ask a clerk if she could buy nylons with the same message embroidered on the tops. The clerk asked if she wanted block letters or script. "Neither," she said. "Just Braille."
> *George Feuermann*

Brevity is the soul of lingerie.
> *Dorothy Parker (1893-1967)*

Work on good prose has three stages: a musical stage when it is composed, an architectural one when it is built, and a textile one when it is woven.
> *Walter Benjamin (1882-1940)*

Few men are of one plain, decided color; most are mixed, shaded and blended, and vary as much, from different situations as changeable silks do from different lights.
> *Lord Chesterfield (1694-1773)*
> *[The technical term for this silk is "changeant". LZ]*

The cardigan is named for James Thomas Brudnell, 7th Earl of Cardigan (1797-1868), who loved to ride wearing a sweater that opened down the front.

Mary had a little lamb
it walked into a pylon
10,000 volts went up its ass
and turned its wool to nylon.

THEATRE (see also ACTORS)

"Hamlet" is a coarse and barbarous play… One might think the work is a product of a drunken savage's imagination.
Voltaire (1694-1778)

If you want to make people weep, you must weep yourself. If you want to make people laugh, your face must remain serious.
Giovanni Jacopo Casanova (1725-1798)

Each work was for me a different kind of failure. And this fact, I guess, put me to writing the next one.
Harold Pinter (1930-   )

The most one can say about our theater, is that it fulfills the essential condition for rebirth: it is dead.
Eric Russell

Drama is life with the dull bits cut out.
Alfred Hitchcock (1899-1980)

An actor is a sculptor who carves in snow.
Edwin Booth (1833-1893)

A drama critic is a man who leaves no turn unstoned.
George Bernard Shaw (1856-1950)

I am enclosing two tickets for the first night of my new play; bring a friend… if you have one.
George Bernard Shaw to Winston Churchill

Cannot possibly attend first night, will attend second… if there is one.
Winston Churchill, in reply

All the world's a stage,
And all the men and women merely players:
They have their exists and their entrances,
And one man in his time plays many parts.
  William Shakespeare (1564-1616)

She runs the gamut of emotions from A to B.
  Dorothy Parker (1893-1967), on Katherine Hepburn

The first theatrical performance on American soil was given in Spanish. Captain Marcos Farfan de los Godos presented a *Comedia* in the Rio Grande near El Paso, on April 30, 1598.

THINKING

Thinking and being are the same thing.
    Parmenides (5th c. BCE)
    [cf. I think, therefore I am of Descartes]

Dubito ergo cogito; cogito ergo sum.
(I doubt, therefore I think; I think, therefore I exist)
    René Descartes (1596-1650)

We are what we think. All that we are is born from our thoughts. With our thoughts we build our world.
    Buddha (563?-453? BCE)

Men are not influenced by things, but by their thoughts about things.
    Epictetus (1st-2nd c.)

Change your thoughts and you change the world.
    Norman Vincent Peale (1898-1983)

Do we ever understand what we think?
    Carl Jung (1875-1961)

For blocks are better cleft with wedges,
Than tools of sharp or softer edges,
And dullest nonsense had been found
By some to be to most profound.
    Samuel Butler (1612-1680)

If I look confused, it's because I'm thinking.
    Samuel Goldwyn (1882-1974)

Struggle against impure thoughts, lest they overcome you. Treat them as they want to treat you, because if you tolerate them, if they take root and grow, know this well, these thoughts will dominate and kill you.
>   *H.P. Blavastsky (1831-1891)*

You can't think and hit at the same time.
>   *Yogi Berra (1925-   )*
>   *[Quite true, also applicable to musicians. Think of Zen. LZ]*

The trouble with talking too fast is you may say something you haven't thought of yet.
>   *Ann Landers (1918-2002)*

Write down the thoughts of the moment. Those that come unsought for are commonly the most valuable.
>   *Francis Bacon (1561-1626)*

Aristotle was famous for knowing everything. He taught that the brain exists merely to cool the blod and is not involved in the process of thinking. This is true only of certain persons.
>   *Will Cuppy (1884-1949)*

Thoughts are like fruit: consume them only when ripe.
>   *Leon Zeldis*

We live physically in the world, mentally in our minds. You don't like living in a dirty home. Avoid, then, dirty thoughts that pollute the mind.
>   *Leon Zeldis*

TIME

Tempus edax rerum
(Time, devourer of all things]
>   *Ovid (43 BCE-18 CE)*

One of the important differences between Israel and the other nations relates to their concept of time. Other nations see time as a straight line without any connection with anything external; one instant of time is not at all similar to another. However, the Torah see time asi a cyclic phenomenon - not a circle but a spiral. In other words, history does repeat itself, to some extent, but at a different level. When we commemorate the anniversary of some event in history, we re-live those aspects in time which created events, and feel anew the associated moods and sensations.

In a sense, we create time, for it is the *Beit Din* [religious tribunal] who declares when it is *Rosh Hodesh* [the new moon]. We are partners in time. We are a people through our calendar, a nation sanctified together with time. A Jewish festival is called a "*moed*", which means "an appointed meeting". Time itself is "*zman*", which means prepared, appointed, set-up. For we are not just remembering and celebrating events of the past; we are touching their present, envisioning and shaping their future.
Mattis Weinberg

Time flies like an arrow
Fruit flies like a banana.
David Eddy

You will never find time for anything. If you want time you must make it.
Charles Buxton (1823-1871)

Don't watch the clock; do what it does: keep going!
Sam Levenson (1911-1980)

To kill time is not murder, it's suicide.
William James (1842-1910)

Time is the coin of your life. It is the only coin you have, and only you can determine how it will be spent. Be careful lest you let other people spend it for you.
Carl Sandburg, poet (1878-1967)

Whoever thinks of going to bed before 12 o'clock is a scoundrel.
Samuel Johnson (1709-1784)

There is no future in time travel.
Howard Griffin (1920-1980)

You cannot kill time without injuring eternity.
Henry David Thoreau (1817-1862)

At a distance, space becomes time and the horizon signifies the future.
Oswald Spengler (1880-1936)

The future influences the present just as much as the past.
Friedrich Nietzsche (1844-1900)

There is only one important moment: the present, and it is important because it is the only time when we have dominion over ourselves.
Leon Tolstoy (1828-1910)

Nothing changes more constantly than the past, for the past that influences our lives does not consist of what actually happened but of what men believe happened.
Gerald W. Johnson (1890-1980)

Radiocarbon dating was discovered by Willard Libby in 1949.
Steven Mithen
[Before then, no accurate dating could be made earlier than the 3rd millennium BCE. LZ]

Lives of great me all remind us
we can make our lives sublime,
and, departing, leave behind us
footprints on the sands of time.
Longfellow (1807-1882)

Men talk of killing time, while time quietly kills them.
Dion Boucicalt

Eternity is a very long time, particularly at the end.
Woody Allen (1935-   )

For the busy person, the day is never long.
Seneca (4 BCE-65 CE)

He that will not apply new remedies must expect new evils, for time is the greatest innovator.
Francis Bacon (1561-1626)

It is futile to talk too much about the past; something like trying to make birth control retroactive.
Charles E. Wilson (1890-1961)

What, of all things in the world, is the longest and the shortest, the swiftest and the slowest, the most divisible and the most extended, the most neglected and the most regretted, without which nothing can be done, which devours all that it little, and enlivens all that is great? Time.
Nothing is longer, since it is the measure of eternity.
Nothing is shorter, since it is insufficient for the accomplishment of our projects.

Nothing is more slow to him that expects; nothing more rapid to him that enjoys.
In greatness it extends to infinity, in smallness to infinitely divisible.
All men neglect it; all regret the loss of time; nothing can be done without it.
It consigns to oblivion whatever is unworthy of being transmitted to posterity, and it immortalizes such actions as are truly great.
Time is man's most precious commodity.

Time is the only non-renewable resource that everybody spends without thought.

Time is the best teacher, unfortunately it kills its students.
Time is a great healer, but it's a lousy beautician.

The word clock comes from the ringing bells (glocken) in the church towers that marked the hours. To distinguish the invariable hours marked by the clock from the variable hours depending on the length of the day, the first were called "of the clock", hence o'clock. Minutes were invented only in 1577 by clockmaker Jost Bürgi (1552-1632), and seconds in 1656, by Christian Huyghens (1629-1695), who invented the pendulum clock based on Galileo's discovery of the simple pendulum. He also founded the wave theory of light.

Time does not exist. The present is a dimensionless edge between an immutable past and the unborn future.
Leon Zeldis

To live looking at the watch stretches the hours and shortens life.
Leon Zeldis

Memories are lifeboats in the shipwreck of time.
Leon Zeldis

TOILET PAPER

The oldest reference to toilet paper appears in a ghost story recorded in the fifth century in China. When a Mr. Yu was using the privy, someone extended his or her arm into the outhouse with a handful of "grass paper" so he could wipe himself.
Charles Benn

TOLERANCE

Tolerance is a social rather than a religious virtue.
   Sir Steven Runciman (1903-2000)

In people as in machines, tolerance permits a maximum of efficiency with a minimum of friction.
   E. J. Lofgren

Excessive tolerance is complicity.
   José Ingenieros (1877-1925)

A thing moderately good is not so good as it ought to be. Moderation in temper is always a virtue, but moderation in principle is always a vice.
   Thomas Paine (1737-1809)

Often, the more you understand, the less you forgive.
   Julian Becker

What is the root cause of intolerance? Ignorance. What and whom you ignore, first you fear, then you hate.
   Leon Zeldis

TONGUE TWISTERS

How much wood could a woodchuck chuck if a woodchuck could chuck wood?

Pablito clavó un clavito, un clavito clavó Pablito. Qué clavito clavó Pablito?

Tres tristes tigres comen un plato de trigo.

TRADITION

Tradition is not an immobile statue, but lives and flows like a powerful river, larger the farther it is from its source. Its content is composed of what the spiritual world has produced.
   G.W.F. Hegel (1770-1831)

It would be foolish to despise tradition. But with our growing self-consciousness and increasing intelligence we must begin to control tradition and assume a critical attitude toward it, if human relations are

ever to change for the better. We must try to recognize what in our accepted tradition is damaging to our fate and dignity – and shape our lives accordingly.
Albert Einstein (1879-1955)

Tradition should be used like a rudder and not as an anchor.

We should act as a boatman, driving the boat forward while looking back.
Leon Zeldis

TRANSLATION

A translation is like a tapestry seen from the back.
Miguel de Cervantes (1547-1616).

A translator is a timid person who, because of his fear, being incapable of contradicting the grammatical rules, puts the translated writer into the prison of ordinary language, betraying him.
José Ortega y Gasset (1883-1955)

It is as impossible to translate poetry as to translate music.
Voltaire (1694-1778)

'Out of sight, out of mind,' when translated into Russian by computer, then back again into English, became 'invisible maniac'.
Arthur Calder-Marshall (1908-1992)

Some poems lose something in the original.
John McInnes

The original is unfaithful to the translation.
Jorge Luis Borges (1899-1986)

Translations, like some women, if beautiful they are not faithful, and if faithful, they are not beautiful.

Goodby, I your new computer translator am.

Translator and counterfeiter are cousins.
Leon Zeldis

TRIVIA

The Wall Street Journal informs us that during his lifetime, a man will shave about 9 meters of beard.
>   *Folha de Sao Paulo, 4.8.96*

The first internal-combustion engine to operate successfully on the four-stroke cycle was built in 1876 by Nicolaus August Otto, a traveling salesman for a wholesale grocer in the Rhineland.

Sir Arthur Conan Doyle, the creator of Sherlock Holmes, was the referee of the 1909 World Heavyweight Boxing Championship.

Omar Khayyam had a big head. When they opened his grave in 1961 to remove his remains to a new mausoleum, they found that the circumference of his skull was 63 centimeters.

TRUTH

Truth is one; sages call it by different names.
>   *Hindu saying*

Amicus Plato sed magis amica veritas.
I'm a friend of Plato, but a greater friend of truth.
>   *Aristotle (384-322 BCE)*

Believe those who are seeking the truth. Doubt those who find it.
>   *André Gide (1969-1951)*

The seal of God is the truth.
>   *Talmud, Shabbat 55b*

Truth rests with God alone, and a little bit with me.
>   *Yiddish proverb*

Divine truths are ever a tetractys, or a triad equal to a tetractys – But the entire scheme is a pentad.
>   *Samuel Taylor Coleridge (1772-1834)*

Facts are not the truth but only indicate where the truth may lie.
>   *Clarence Barron (1855-1928)*

Convictions are more dangerous to truth than lies.
>   *Nietzsche (1844-1900)*

I would give my life for a man searching for the truth, but I would kill a man who believes he has found it.
Luis Buñuel (1900-1983)

Truth is not discovered but invented. Therefore, it is always provisional, existing as long as it is not refuted.
Karl Popper (1902-1994)

It is one of the maladies of our age to profess a frenzied allegiance to truth in unimportant matters, but to refuse consistently to face her when graver issues are at hand.
Janos Arany (1817-1882)

Truth is beautiful, without doubt, but so are lies.
Ralph Waldo Emerson (1803-1882)

The road to truth is long, and lined the entire way with annoying bastards.
Alexander Jablokov (1956-   )

There is no worse lie than a truth misunderstood by those who hear it.
William James (1842-1910)

Truth is the most valuable thing we have. Let us economize it.
Mark Twain (1835-1910)

A little inaccuracy sometimes saves tons of explanations.
Saki (H. H. Munro) (1870-1916)

No pleasure is comparable to standing upon the vantage ground of truth... and to see the errors, and wanderings, and mists, and tempests, in the vale below.
Francis Bacon (1561-1626)

There is no power that can transform a thing into something it is not.
Blaise Pascal (1623-1662)

The study of error serves as a stimulating introduction to the study of truth.
Walter Lippmann (1889-1974)

I don't want any yes-men around me. I want everubody to tell me the truth, even if it costs them their jobs.
Sam Goldwyn (1882-1974)

The True is the identification of appearance and reality.
   Alfred North Whitehead (1861-1947)

All err more dangerously because each follows a truth. Their mistake lies not in following a falsehood but in following another truth.
   Blaise Pascal (1623-1662)

The least initial deviation from truth is multiplied later a thousand-fold.
   Aristotle (384-322 BC)

The English are polite by telling lies. The Americans are polite by telling the truth.
   Malcolm Bradbury (1932-2000)

The cruelest lies are often told in silence.
   Robert Louis Stevenson (1850-1894)

Truth is not only violated by falsehood; it may be equally outraged by silence.
   Henri F. Amiel (1821-1881)

The world always makes the assumption that the exposure of an error is identical with the discovery of truth - that the error and truth are simply opposite. They are nothing of the sort. What the world turns to, when it is cured on one error, is usually simply another error, and maybe one worse than the first one.
   H. L. Mencken (1880-1956)

No one lies so boldly as the man who is indignant.
   Friedrich Nietzsche (1844-1900)

Vilify! Vilify! Some of it will always stick.
   Beaumarchais (1732-1799)
   [Goebbels implemented this policy, and so does the PLO. LZ]

I never did give anybody hell. I just told the truth and they thought it was hell.
   Harry S. Truman (1884-1972)

A lie can travel half way around the world while the truth is putting on its shoes.
   Mark Twain (1835-1910)

As scarce as truth is, the supply has always exceeded the demand.

230

T-SHIRTS

I don't suffer from insanity. I enjoy every minute of it.

You're just jealous because the voices only talk to me.

I'm not a comple idiot; some parts are missing.

I want to die in my sleep like my grandfather – not screaming and yelling like the passengers in his car.

I took an IQ test and the results were negative.

Ever stop to think and forgot to start again?

Procrastinate...NOW

Rehab is for quitters.

Arkansas: one million people and fifteen last names.

Failure is not an option. It comes bundled with the software.

Stupidity is not a handicap. Park elsewhere!

Ham and eggs – a day's work for the chicken, a lifetime commitment for the pig.

Welcome to Kentucky – Set your watch back 20 years.

Stress is when you wake up screaming and then you realize you haven't fallen asleep yet.

Brain cells come and brain cells go, but fat cells live forever.

Strike out and eliminate redundancy.

Why is it that our children can't read a Bible in school, but they can in prison?

UNDERSTANDING

Understanding others is wisdom, understanding oneself is illumination. He who conquers others is strong, but he who conquers himself is powerful.

Lao Tsu (604?-531?)

I don't know how to overcome others. All that I know is how to overcome myself.

Yagiu

UNKNOWN

Writing his book on algebra, Omar Khayam used the Arab word *shay*, which means thing, to represent an unknown quantity. The word could also be written *xay*. Replaced by its first letter, x became the universal sign of an unknown quantity.

Amin Maalouf (1949-   )

The notion of primitive man possessing some inner peace which we civilized people have somehow lost, and need to regain, is a lot of nonesense. Your average New Guinea native lives not only in fear of his enemies, but in terror-struck dread of the unknown.
Gordon Linsley

They are ill discoverers that think there is no land, when they can see nothing but sea.
Francis Bacon (1561-1626)

UTOPIA

Don't tell me about the ideal society: there have to be at least two; otherwise all history and social science is nonsense.
Franz Baermann Steiner

Hell is like Utopia, but with central heating.

VANITY

No place affords a more striking conviction of the vanity of human hopes than a public library; for who can see the wall crowded on every side by mighty volumes, the works of laborious meditations and accurate inquiry, now scarcely known but by the catalogue.
Dr. Samuel Johnson (1707-1996)

Pride does not wish to owe and vanity does not wish to pay.
La Rochefoucauld (1613-1680)

She got her looks from her father. He's a plastic surgeon.
Groucho Marx (1890-1977)

VICES

After vices got the name of virtue, propriety was lost.
Seneca (4 BCE- 65 CE)

There are vices of the times and vices of the individual
Francis Bacon (1561-1626)

A thing moderately good is not so good as it ought to be. Moderation in temper is always a virtue, but moderation in principle is always a vice.
Thomas Paine (1737-1809)

Never trust a man who has not a single redeeming vice.
Winston Churchill (1874-1965)

He has all the virtues I dislike and none of the vices I admire.
Winston Churchill (1874-1965)

Vice is a monster of so frightful mien,
as, to be hated, needs but to be seen;
yet seen too oft, familiar with her face,
we first endure, then pity, then embrace.
Alexander Pope (1688-1744)

Malice is a greater magnifying glass than kindness.
Marquis of Halifax (1633-1695)

Until 1533, sodomy was not a crime in Common Law in England; Only the 'Act for the Punishment of the Vice of Buggery' of 1533-34 made it a capital offence.

Sloth is the mother of all vices, and as a mother, we must respect her.

VICTORY

Each victory is the summary of many defeats.
Osvaldo Rossler

Rarely has desperation failed to bring about victory.
Simón Bolivar (1783-1830)

Those who know how to win are much more numerous than those who know how to make proper use of their victories.
Polybius (205?125? BCE)

You may have to fight a battle more than once to win it.
Margaret Thatcher (1925-)

VIRTUE

To many people virtue consists chiefly in repenting faults, not in avoiding them.
Georg Christoph Lichtenberg (1742-1799)

There is only one path of Virtue,
all other paths are no paths.
> *The Avesta*

The highest qualities often unfit a man for society. We don't take ingots
with us to market, we take silver or small change.
> *Sébastien Chamfort (1741-1794)*

Hypocricy is the homage which vice pays to virtue.
> *La Rochefoucauld (1613-1680)*

Men's virtues have their seasons even as fruits have.
> *La Rochefoucauld (1613-1680)*

Rarely do great beauty and great virtue dwell together.
> *Francesco Petrarca (1304-1374)*

Virtues, like essences, lose their fragrance when exposed.
> *William Shenstone*

Real unselfishness consists in sharing the interests of others.
> *George Santayana (1863-1952)*

Don't trust first impulses; they are always generous.
> *Talleyrand (1754-1838)*

Nature does not bestow virtue; to be good is an art.
> *Seneca (4 BCE-65 CE)*

The strength of a man's virtue should not be measured by his special
exertions, but by his habitual acts.
> *Blaise Pascal (1623-1662)*

We ought to remember that virtue is not hereditary.
> *Thomas Paine (1737-1809)*

VISITORS

Visitors always give pleasure - if not the arrival, the departure.
> *Portuguese proverb*

Some cause happiness wherever they go; others whenever they go.
> *Oscar Wilde (1854-1900)*

I have had a perfectly wonderful evening. But this wasn't it.
    Groucho Marx (1895-1977)

WAR   *see also:* **APPEASEMENT, GENERALS**

I fear our own mistakes more than anything the enemy may devise.
    Pericles (d. 429 BCE)

In order to have good soldiers, a nation must be always at war.
    Napoleon Bonaparte (1769-1821)

Decadence is the essential condition of a society which believes it has
evolved to the point where it will never have to go to war.
    Robert D. Kaplan (1952-   )

The art of war consists in disposing your troops in such a manner they
may be in all places at the same time.
    Napoleon Bonaparte (1769-1821)

As a rule, in a battle one uses normal force to engage into combat, and use
extraordinary force to gain victory.
    Sun Tzu (c. 544-496 BCE)

Force and fraud are in war the two cardinal virtues.
    Thomas Hobbes (1588-1679)

In time of war the loudest patriots are the greatest profiteers.
    August Bebel (1840-1913)

War is a thundercloud where brightness floats blacker than the night.
    Victor Hugo (1802-1885)

How is the world governed and how do wars begin? Diplomats tell lies to
journalists and believe them when they see them in print.
    Karl Kraus (1874-1936)

No state at war with another should engage in hostilities of such kind as
to render mutual confidence impossible when peace will have to be made.
    Immanuel Kant (1724-1804)

War hath no fury like a noncombatant
    C.E. Montague (1867-1928)

They have not wanted 'Peace' at all; they have wanted to be spared war – as though the absence of war was the same as peace.
  Dorothy Thompson (1893-1961)

Peace is not made around the council table, or in treaties, but in the hearts of men and women.
  Herbert Hoover (1874-1964)

Was is an ugly thing, but not the ugliest of things; the decayed and degraded state of moral and patriotic feeling which thinks that nothing is worth war is much worse. A man who has nothing for which he is willing to fight, nothing he cares about more than his own personal safety, is a miserable creature who has no chance of being free, unless made and kept so by the exertions of better persons than himself.
  John Stuart Mill (1806-1873)

A soldier who runs away is good for another war.
  Italian proverb

The object of war is not to die for your country but to make the other bastard die for his.
  General George Patton (1885-1945)

An infallible method of conciliating a tiger is to allow onself to be devoured.
  Konrad Adenauer (1876-1967)

No protracted war can fail to endanger the freedom of a democratic country.
  Alexis de Tocqueville (1805-1859)

Join the army, see the world, meet interesting people, kill them.

In 1914 the German army destroyed the university library at Louvain, which had no military significance. 300,000 volumes were lost, including 1,000 incunabula and 800 illuminated manuscripts. In 1992, the Serbs assaulted the National Library in Sarajevo, destroying almost all of its 1.5 million books.

Total casualties at Borodino are calculated at about 73,000 while casualties at Waterloo were about 63,000 men.
  Times Literary Supplement, 21.5.2004, p. 26

WEALTH see RICHES

WILDE, OSCAR

He was a man who had so many different personalities that he could only ever be true to himself when he was inconsistent.
> *Thomas Wright*

Given a choice of alternatives, Wilde always managed to choose both.
> *Richard Ellmann (1918-1987)*

Wilde is engaged in a furious war against morality.
> *Thomas Mann (1875-1955)*

WINE

The ability of alcohol to kill bacteria and parasites made it safer in antiquity to drink wine rather than water. Unadulterated wine was so scarce, however, that Ovid and Horace compared pure wine with virgin girls.
> *Henry Hobhouse (1854-1937)*

WISDOM

Wisdom is not a station to arrive at, but the manner of traveling.
> *Anthony de Mello (1931-1987)*

Three things it is best to avoid: a strange dog, a flood, and a man who thinks he is wise.
> *Welsh proverb*

Nobody is so wise that has nothing to learn,and nobody is so ignorant that has nothing to teach.
> *Johann G. Fichte (1762-1814)*

Great minds have purposes; others have wishes.
> *Washington Irving (1783-1859)*

Wisdom too often never comes, and so one ought not to reject it merely because it comes late.
> *Justice Felix Frankfurter (1882-1965)*

The intelligent man finds almost everything ridiculous; the sensible man hardly anything.
Goethe (1749-1832)

You can tell whether a man is clever by his answers. You can tell whether a man is wise by his questions.
Naguib Mahfouz (1911-2006)

When head and heart are opposed, the heart is the one that makes the decision; the poor head will always give up, even though it is the wiser.
Paul Heyse (1830-1914)

The Arctic expresses the sum of all wisdom: Silence.
Walter Bauer (1877-1960)

Nothing is more harmful to a nation, as clever people who pass as intelligent.
Francis Bacon (1561-1626)

In seeking wisdom, the first step is silence, the second listening, the third remembering, the fourth practicing, the fifth: teaching others.
Solomon Ibn Gabirol (c. 1022-1058)

It takes a wise man to discover a wise man.
Xenophanes (c. 570-476 BCE)

We learn wisdom from failure much more than from success. We often discover what will do by finding out what will not do, and probably he who never made a mistake never made a discovery.
Samuel Smiles (1812-1904)

By three methods we may learn wisdom: first, by reflection, which is noblest; second, by imitation, which is the easiest; and third, by experience, which is the bitterest.
Confucius (551-479 BCE)

A single conversation across the table with a wise man is worth a month's study of books.
Chinese proverb

Wisdom comes with winter.
Oscar Wilde (1854-1900)

A wise man knows everything; a shrewd one, everybody.

Wisdom is expressed not in words but in actions.

It is easier to put on slippers than to carpet the whole world.

The beginning of wisdom is the definition of terms.

WIT

Brevity is the soul of wit.
William Shakespeare (1564-1616)

Wit is educated insolence.
Aristotle (384-322 BCE)

Never get into a battle of wits with unarmed opponents.
Allen Roberts (1917-1997)

Some men have acted courage who had it not, but no man can act wit.
Marquis of Halifax (1633-1695)

You can pretend to be serious; you can't pretend to be witty.
Sacha Guitry (1885-1957)

Wit is the salt of conversation, not the food.
William Hazlitt (1778-1830)

Many get the name for being witty, only to lose the credit of being sensible.
Gracian (1601-1658)

Seriousness is the only refuge of the shallow.
Oscar Wilde (1854-1900)

I would horse-whip you… if I had a horse.
Groucho Marx (1890-1977)

WITCHES

Between the fifteenth and eighteenth centuries, on a conservative estimate, some 40,000 people, four out of five of them women, were executed in Europe as witches.
Nathan Johnstone

In 1486, *Malleus Maleficarum* included reports of men whose penises had been stolen by witches. One of the remedies to cure impotence was urinating through the keyhole of the church where the couple had married.
>   *Catherine Rider*

I don't believe in ghosts, but I'm scared of them.
>   *Mme. de Deffand (1697-1780)*

I don't believe in witches, but there are some.
>   *[Spanish proverb: Yo no creo en las brujas, pero que las hay, las hay]*

The English like to hunt foxes; Americans hunt witches. Since none are to be found, they invent them, giving them different names every time.
>   *Leon Zeldis*

WIVES see also MARRIAGE

Wives are young men's mistresses, companions for middle age, and old men's nurses.
>   *Francis Bacon (1561-1626)*

Heckler: "Mr. Churchill, if I were your wife, I would poison your coffee!"
Churchill: "Madam, if you were my wife, I would drink it."
>   *Winston Churchill (1874-1965)*

My wife keeps complaining I never listen to her… or something like that.

WOMEN

Women who want to be equal to men have no ambition.
>   *Timothy Leary (192-1996)*

Whatever women do they must do twice as well as men to be thought half as good. Luckily this is not too difficult.
>   *Charlotte Whitton (1896-1975)*

If men could get pregnant, abortion would be a sacrament.
>   *Florynce Kenndy (1916-2000)*

Brigands demand your money or your life; women required both.
>   *Nicholas Murray Butler (1862-1947)*

Some ladies pursue culture in bands, as though it were dangerous to meet it alone.
Edith Wharton (1862-1937)

Women should be obscene and not heard.
Groucho Marx (1890-1977)

When women love us, they forgive everything, even our crimes, but when they do not love us, they give us credit for nothing, not even our virtues.
Honoré de Balzac (1799-1850)

A virtuous woman has in her heart a fiber less or more than other women: she's stupid or sublime.
Honoré de Balzac (1799-1850)

Women would be more charming if we could fall into her arms without falling into her hands.
Ambrose Bierce (1842-1914?)

Choose a woman of whom you can say: I could have chosen a more beautiful one, but not a better one.
Pythagoras (d. 497 BCE)

I like to look at bright men and listen to beautiful women.
Oscar Wilde (1854-1900)

A woman undressing, how dazzling. It is like the sun piercing the clouds.
Auguste Rodin (1840-1917)

The breast is second only to God.
Dogon proverb

The most powerful hydraulic force in the universe is the tear of a woman.
Carlos Fisas

In mixed company, women practice a sort of visual shorthand, which later, they will laboriously and at great length decode in the company of other women.
Malcolm de Chazal (1902-1981)

On one issue at least, men and women agree; they both distrust women.
H. L. Mencken (1880-1956)

The great question that has never been answered, and which I have not yet been able to answer despite my thirty years of research into the feminine soul, is: what does a woman want?
  Sigmund Freud (1856-1939)

What do women want? Shoes.
  Mimi Pond

A woman must be loved, not understood. That's the first thing to understand.
  Osho (1931-1990)

Between a woman's yes and a no,
there is no room for a pin to go.
(*Entre el Sí y el No de la mujer, no me atrevería yo a poner una punta de alfiler*).
  Miguel de Cervantes (1547-1616)

Feminine passion is to masculine as an epic to an epigram.
  Karl Kraus (1874-1936)

Women like desperate men; if they don't find them, they make them.
  Leon Daudet (1867-1942)

Boys like to play with soldiers, and girls with dolls. When they grow up, it's the other way around.
  Nina Yomerowska

The years that a woman subtracts from her age are not lost. They are added to another woman's.
  Diane de Poitiers (1499-1566)

I have heard with admiring submission the experience of a lady who declared that the sense of being well-dressed gives a feeling of inward tranquility, which religion is powerless to bestow.
  Ralph Waldo Emerson (1803-1882)

A woman is like a tea bag. You don't know how strong it is till it's in hot water.
  Eleanor Roosevelt (1884-1962)

When women kiss it always reminds me of prizefighters shaking hands.
  Henry Louis Mencken (1880-1956)

Behave towards your wife as you would to another's.
Jean Giraudoux (1882-1944)

No woman ever hates a man for being in love with her, but many a woman hates a man for being a friend to her.
Alexander Pope (1688-1744)

A woman is always buying something.
Ovid (43 BCE - 18 CE)

If women did not exist, money would have no meaning.
Aritoteles Onassis (1906-1975)

Women prefer men who have something tender about them – especially the legal kind.
Kay Ingram

In order to avoid being called a flirt, she always yielded easily.
Charles, Count Talleyrand (1754-1838)

Women are the wild life of a country; morality corresponds to game laws.

A woman worries about the future until she gets a husband. A man never worries about the future until he gets a wife.

If a man is forceful and is aggressive, he is perceived as dynamic, a leader, he is a "visionary". A woman who does the same things is a bitch.

WORDS

Dictionary: Opinions presented as truth in alphabetical order.
John Ralston Saul (1947-   )

Words fascinate me. They always have. For me, browsing in a dictionary is like being turned loose in a bank.
Eddie Cantor (1892-1964)

The difference between the right word and the almost right word is the difference between lightning and a lightning rod.
Mark Twain (1835-1910)

Words, like eyeglasses, obscure everything they do not make clear.
Joseph Joubert (1754-1824)

Words are no good to feel the secret. Who can give name and surname to the infinite?
  Huang Ta Chung

When ideas fail, words come in very handy.
  Wolfgang Goethe (1749-1832)

Words are chameleons, which reflect the color of their environment.
  Learned Hand (1872-1961)

No one means all he says, and yet very few say all they mean, for words are slippery and thought is viscous.
  Henry Brooks Adams (1838-1918)

Wolof (a West African language that came to the US with the slaves) has given the following words to hip talk: 'hip' comes from *hipikat*, a sage or knowing fellow, 'dig' from *deg* or *dega*, to understand; 'bug' from *bugal*, to annoy.
  Times Literary Supplement, 15.12.2000, p. 14

Joseph Hooker, a Civil War general, provided his troops with professional ladies of easy virtue when soldiers were bored in camp and in need of stimulus, and thus provided a synonym for "prostitute". Rubber got its name from its use as an eraser.
  Henry Hobhouse (1854-1937)

Antanaclasis: a form of speech in which a key word is repeated and used in a different, and sometimes contrary way, as in "our frequent fliers can frequent other fliers" (British Airways).
  James H. Leigh (1952-   )

It's a damn poor mind that can only think of one way to spell a word.
  Andrew Jackson (1767-1845)

Words are slippery and thought is viscous.
  Henry Adam

If lawyers are disbarred and clergymen defrocked, doesn't it follow that electricians can be delighted; musicians denoted; cowboys deranged; models deposed; tree surgeons debarked and drycleaners depressed?
  Virginia Ostman

Chiasmus: a reversal of the order of words in two otherwise parallel phrases (e.g. Don't count the passing days; make the passing days count).

Dawn: Lucid order dawns;
                And as from Chaos old the jarring seeds
                Of nature at the voice divine repair'd
                Each to its place, till rosy earth unveil'd
                Her fragrant bosom, and the joyful sun
                Sprung up the blue serene.
    Mark Akenside (1721-1770)

Phudnik: a nudnik with a PhD.

The word "scientist" was invented only in 1833 by William Whewell, an English popularizer of science.
The cardigan is named for James Thomas Brudnell, 7th Earl of Cardigan (1797-1868), who loved to ride wearing a sweater that opened down the front.

Blue Laws: Connecticut laws against Sabbath-breaking, blasphemy and drinking were printed on blue paper.

The sandwich is named after John Montagu, 4th Earl of Sandwich (1718-1792), an inveterate gambler who preferred to eat at the gaming table so he would not miss any play.

Rebarbative: repellent, irritating.
    [Why is a beard irritating? The French thought so. I wonder what they put their heads into close contact with. LZ]

No word in the English language rhymes with month, orange, silver or purple.

"The quick brown fox jumps over the lazy dog" uses every letter of the alphabet.

Ephemera: minor transient documents of everyday life.

In Maori there are almost forty words for a spear.

The Greek word for word is now a word for visual trademarks (*logos*).

Verecund: bashful, modest.

And a couple that would not get into the dictionary:

Diagnostic: someone who doesn't believe in two gods.

The plural of octopus: hexadecipus.

Avoid ambiguity, except in certain cases.
  Leon Zeldis

WORDS INTO ACTION

Words are also actions, and actions are a kind of words.
  Ralph Waldo Emerson (1803-1882)

Speech is conveniently located midway between thought and action, where it often substitutes for both.
  John Andrew Holmes

As I grow older, I pay less attention to what men say. I just watch what they do.
  Andrew Carnegie (1835-1919)

Five frogs are sitting on a log. Four decide to jump off. How many are left? Answer: five, because there is a difference between deciding and doing.
  Mark. L. Feldman & Michael F. Spratt

It is nice to make heroic decisions and to be prevented by 'circumstances beyond your control' from ever trying to execute them.
  William James (1842-1910)

I hear and I forget. I see and I remember. I do and I understand.
  Confucius (551-479 BCE)

Thought is the blossom; language the bud; action the fruit behind it.
  Ralph Waldo Emerson (1803-1882)

He who desires but acts not, breeds pestilence.
  William Blake (1757-1827)

It is by acts and not by ideas that people live.
  Anatole France (1844-1924)

Let him that would move the world first move himself.
>*Socrates (469-399 BCE)*

There is a law in psychology that if you form a picture in your mind of what you would like to be, and you keep and hold that picture there long enough, you will soon become exactly as you have been thinking.
>*William James, (1842 – 1910)*

He who does right is better than he who thinks right.
>*Albert Pike (1809-1891)*

The proliferation of competitive discourses on revolution [in France] spirals inevitably towards massacre.
>*Patrice Gueniffey*

Slanderous talk is like the sharp arrows of the warrior (Psalm 120:4). This is explained, because all other weapons smite from close quarters, while the arrow smites from the distance. It is spoken in Rome and kills in Syria.
>*Midrash - see also* **EVIL**

When you say that you agree to a thing on principle, you mean that you have not the slightest intention of carrying it out in practice.
>*Otto von Bismark (1815-1898)*

You would be surprised how hard it often is to translate an action into thought.
>*Karl Kraus (1874-1936)*

We are all inclined to judge ourselves by our ideals; others by their acts.
>*Harold Nicholson (1886-1968)*

If you feel strongly about graffiti, sign a partition.

After all is said and done, more is said than done.

Diogenes, the famous Cynic philosopher, wanted to live with the greatest frugality, yet he counterfeited Greek coins.
>*Leon Zeldis*

WORK

Work is where we engage with the world, meet its resistance, obey its reality, change it. Work is thoroughly real... Participation in work, imaginative and practical, joins person to person in community.
>*John Ruskin (1819-1900)*

We all have a basic need to be active, engaged in meaningful pursuits, and valued by other people. In an important sense, these things constitute the true value of work more than money or power.
Brad Edmunson

All paid jobs absorb and degrade the mind.
Aristotle (384-322 BCE)

The workman who wants to make his work well must begin by sharpening his tools.
Confucius (551-479 BCE)

I slept and dreamt that life was joy. I awoke and found that life was duty. I worked and, behold, duty is joy.
Rabindranath Tagore (1861-1941)

Pray as if everything depended upon God and work as if everything depended upon man.
Francis Cardinal Spellman (1889-1967)

I have never liked working. To me a job is an invasion of privacy.
Danny McGoorty

It is not work that kills men, it's worry.
Henry Ward Beecher (1813-1887)
[but some executives worry about work. LZ]

Work is the curse of the drinking classes.
Oscar Wilde (1854-1900)

No other technique for the conduct of life attaches the individual so firmly to reality as laying emphasis on work; for his work at least gives him a secure place in a portion of reality, in the human community.
Sigmund Freud (1856-1939)

Work never killed anyone, but why take chances?

There are two words that will open many doors: 'Push' and 'Pull'.

WORLD

The world is all that is the case.
Wittgenstein (1889-1951)

248

If the world were merely seductive, that would be easy. If it were merely challenging, that would be no problem. But I arise in the morning torn between a desire to improve the world and a desire to enjoy the world. That makes it hard to plan the day.
E. B. White (1899-1985)

Every man who has seen the world nows that nothing is so useless as a general axiom.
Thomas Babbington Macaulay (1800-1859).

I've come to believe that the whole world is an enigma, a harmless enigma that is made terrible by our own mad attempt to interpret it as though it had an underlying truth.
Umberto Eco (1932-   )

Maybe this world is another planet's hell.
Aldous Huxley (1894-1963)

The whole problem with the world is that fools and fanatics are always so certain of their ideas, while wiser people are so full of doubts.
Bertrand Russell (1872-1970)

Change your thoughts and you change the world.
Norman Vincent Peale (1898-1993)

The world is a comedy to those that think, a tragedy to those that feel.
Horace Walpole (1717-1797)

There is a better world, but it's very expensive.

Improving the world is beyond the powers of most men, but improving oneself, everybody can do.
Leon Zeldis

WORRY

Worry a little every day and in a lifetime you will lose a couple of years. If something is wrong, fix it if you can. But train yourself not to worry. Worry never fixes anything.
Mary Hemingway (1946-1961)

It is not work that kills men, it's worry.
>   *Henry Ward Beecher (1813-1887)*
>   *[but some executives reply: true enough, but nothing worries me so much as work.* Factory Management and Maintenance, *February 1955]*

WRITERS AND WRITING

Quel homme aurait été Balzac s'il eut su écrire.
What a man would Balzac had been, had he known how to write.
>   *Gustave Flaubert (1821-1880)*

Crude, immoral, vulgar and senseless.
>   *Leon Tolstoy (1828-1910) on Shakespeare*
>   *[He also considered Nietzsche to be stupid and abnormal]*

Malicious, envious, debauched.
>   *Nikolai Strakhov (Dostoievsky's first biographer)(1828- ?) on Dostoievsky.*

A drunken philosopher who wrote only when intoxicated.
>   *Voltaire (1694-1778), on Rabelais*

"Hamlet" is a coarse and barbarous play. One might think the work is the product of a drunken savage's imagination.
>   *Voltaire (1694-1778)*

[Henry James] had a mind so fine that no idea could violate it.
>   *T. S. Eliot (1888-1965)*

Some editors are failed writers, but so are most writers.
>   *T. S. Eliot (1888-1965)*

Ernest Hemingway is a guy who keeps saying the same thing over and over until you begin to believe that it must be good.
>   *Raymond Chandler (1888-1959)*

Hemingway was a jerk.
>   *Harold Robbins (1916-1997)*

He has never been known to use a word that might send a reader to the dictionary.
>   *William Faulkner (1897-1962), about Ernest Hemingway*

Poor Faulkner. Does he really think big emotions come from big words?
Ernest Hemingway (1899-1961), about William Faulkner

A good way to start a library is to leave out the works of Jane Austen.
Mark Twain (1835-1910)

The mama of dada.
Clifton Fadiman (1904-1999), about Gertrude Stein

There are really only two stories: either you go on a journey, or a stranger comes to town.
John Gardner (1926-2007)

You think of something, beging to write, and end up writing something quite different from what you were thinking before.
Miguel de Unamuno (1864-1936)

Those authors I can never love
who write 'it fit him like a glove'.
Though baseballs may be hit, not 'hitted',
the past of fit is always fitted.
Ogden Nash (1902-1971)

Writers, like teeth, are divided into incisors and grinders.
Walter Bagehot (1826-1877)

Work on good prose has three stages: a musical stage when it is composed, an architectural one when it is built, and a textile one when it is woven.
Walter Benjamin (1882-1940)

A well-written life is almost as rare as a well-spent one.
Thomas Carlyle (1795-1881)

Scribbling seems to be a sort of symptom of an unruly age.
Montaigne (1533-1592)

No man but a blockhead ever wrote, except for money.
Dr. Samuel Johnson (1709-1784)

The profession of book-writing makes horse racing seem like a solid, stable business.
John Steinbeck (1902-1968)

I don't know up to what point a writer can be a revolutionary. A writer works with language, which belongs to tradition.
Jorge Luis Borges (1899-1986)

Sperone-Speroni explains very well why a writer's form of expression may seem quite clear to him yet obscure to the reader; the reader is advancing from language to thought, the writer from thought to language.
Sébastien Chamfort (1741-1794)

It's the reader who writes the book, and not the writer.
Paul Auster (1947-   )

Every style that is not boring is a good one.
Voltaire (1694-1778)

To write simply is as difficult as to be good.
Somerset Maugham (1874-1965)

Your manuscript is both good and original, but the part that is good is not original, and the part that is original is not good.
Samuel Johnson (1709-1784)

The difference between journalism and literature is that journalism is unreadable and literature is not read.
Oscar Wilde (1854-1900)

I can write about something that happened yesterday, but that is journalism. And this is, for me, actually, the difference between literature and journalism. Or between an article and a novel, to be more precise.
Gabriel García Márquez (1928-   )

Times are bad. Children no longer obey their parents and everyone is writing a book.
Marcus Tullius Cicero (106-43 BCE)

The written word is a poor substitute for conversation.
Oscar Wilde (1854-1900)

The wastebasket is a writer's best friend.
Isaac Bashevis Singer (1904-1991)

I love deadlines. I love the whooshing sound they make as they fly by.
Douglas Adams (1952-2001)

Genuinely good remarks surprise their author as well as his audience.
> *Joseph Joubert (1754-1824)*

He wrapped himself in quotations, as a beggar would enfold himself in the purple of Emperors.
> *Rudyard Kipling (1865-1936)*

The man who is asked by an author what he thinks of his work is put to the torture and is not obliged to speak the truth.
> *Dr. Samuel Johnson (1709-1784)*

An editor should have a pimp for a brother, so he'd have someone to look up to.
> *Gene Fowler (1890-1960)*

An avowed admirer of brevity, Erasmus was one of the most prolific writers of all time. His *De copia* is an eulogy for long-windedness, and his paraphrases of the New Testament are often far longer than the original.
> *Alastair Hamilton*

Thank you for sending me a copy of your book. I'll waste no time reading it.
> *Moses Hadas (1900-1966)*

Though he has tortured the English language, he has not succeeded in forcing it to reveal his meaning.

A manuscript, like a foetus, is never improved by showing it to somebody before it is completed.

Originality is the art of concealing your sources.

Creativity is great, but plagiarism is faster.

YEAR

Come, cheer up, my lads! 'tis to glory we steer
To add something more to this wonderful year.
> *David Garrick (1717-1779)*

A lifetime should not be counted in years but in days.
> *Leon Zeldis*

YOUTH

The days of our youth are the days of our glory... What are garlands and crowns to the brow that is wrinkled?
> *Lord Byron (1788-1824)*

I am not young enough to know everything.
> *James M. Barrie (1860-1937)*

To be adult is to be alone.
> *Jean Rostand (1894-1977)*

Some people say that I must be a horrible person, but that's not true. I have the heart of a young boy – in a jar on my desk.
> *Steven King (1947-   )*

You are only young once, but you can be immature all your life.

If youth knew, if old age could.

Leon Zeldis

León Zeldis was born in Buenos Aires, son of Russian immigrants who escaped from the Bolshevik revolution. A few months after his birth, the family moved to Valparaiso, Chile, where he grew up. He studied Textile Engineering at the University of Philadelphia (USA), and after returning to Chile he taught at the State Technical University of Santiago. He married Luisa Drapkin and after their four children were born they moved to Israel, where they live until now.

Zeldis has published hundreds of articles and stories in English and Spanish, two collections of poems and a book of short stories in Spanish, a novel in English, *Land of Four Seas*, and 10 books on Freemasonry.

During the 1970's he took up painting and held several exhibitions. Recently he published a book-catalog with some of his paintings.

He has been an active Freemason since 1959, reached some of the highest positions in Israeli Freemasonry, served for many years as Editor of *The Israeli Freemason*.

He is a member of many Masonic bodies, and is frequently invited to lecture abroad on Masonic history, symbolism and philosophy.

Zeldis is a member of Mensa, and also served for 45 years as Honorary Consul of Chile in Tel Aviv. The Chilean Government awarded him the Order Bernardo O'Higgins.

Among other hobbies, he and his wife love classical music and they collect folk musical instruments.

www.ingramcontent.com/pod-product-compliance
Lightning Source LLC
Chambersburg PA
CBHW031427270326
41930CB00007B/600